ENDORSEMENTS

"This book by Minister Kevin takes me back to my childhood when I found out about hell and how the fear of going there led me to take the walk down the aisle to give my heart to the Lord. I'm sure that reading this book will have the same influence on anyone who isn't aware of the punishment for anyone who hasn't given their heart to our Savior. The book was amazing. Bottom line this book is a life-changer. I love the cover. It should create a great deal of interest. I think you've got a big-seller there that's sure to be a blessing to many."

—Garry "G" Cobb

Former Philadelphia Eagle & Dallas Cowboy, 610 WIP All Sports Radio Analyst & CBS Radio

Philadelphia, Pennsylvania

"Minister Benton navigates readers through a divine illustration of his life which exemplifies persecution and perseverance; love, honor, and integrity. *'A Field Trip to Hell'* tugged at my emotions, transcended my knowledge of hell, and ministered the Word of God to me. My mind is renewed after reading this book. It's truly a masterpiece."

—Gerald Jordan MS,

Former Los Angeles Lakers & Harlem Globetrotter

Philadelphia, Pennsylvania

"This book is very, very good and it's actually two books in one with all the testimonies. I could not stop reading it; I could not put it down."

—Michal Curry,

Praise Coordinator for WGTW-TV27
Trinity Broadcasting Network

Folcroft, Pennsylvania

"Over the years in book publishing, I have worked on many books signaling the end of the world and accounting for the ultimate destiny of humankind. Many of these books have been effective in detailing the coming days of both prosperity and disasters of epic proportion. Few of them, however, have been as fascinating, poignant, and instructional as Minister Kevin Benton's, 'A Field Trip to Hell.' This book is a great tool for those needing a practical way to inform unbelievers (and even believers) of the realities of hell, and a practical way of witnessing to them.

Endorsements

God has not given us a spirit of fear, but we should all have a proper fear of going to hell."

—Leonard G. Goss,

GoodEditors.com

Valparaiso, Indiana

"After reading the chapter in the book that takes readers on the actual field trip to hell, I must admit that I have never read anything quite like it. There is a nearly universal curiosity or fascination about hell that will attract a wide range of media attention. This attraction stretches across Christian and non-Christian audiences. It is one of a kind and I hope it ends up on the bestseller list."

—Greg D. Foster,

Literary Agent and Consultant

Van Wert, Ohio

"Minister Kevin Benton writes his story with heartfelt conviction and realism. By sharing experiences from his personal life, Kevin reveals insights and scriptural truths that will impact every reader. Taking his 'Field Trip to Hell' is genuinely a life-changing event."

—Claire Diamond

Liberty University Press

Lynchburg, Virginia

"After speaking with Kevin, I was amazed to hear that this was his first book. I think you found your calling, Mr. Benton. God works in mysterious ways. You think your mind, body and spirit is built for one dream you have been chasing your whole life, then the curve ball hits the mitt and divine intervention starts to take place. Can't wait for the follow up. Great work."

—Troy Price

Blazonco Website Designer

San Clemente, California

a FIELD TRIP to HELL

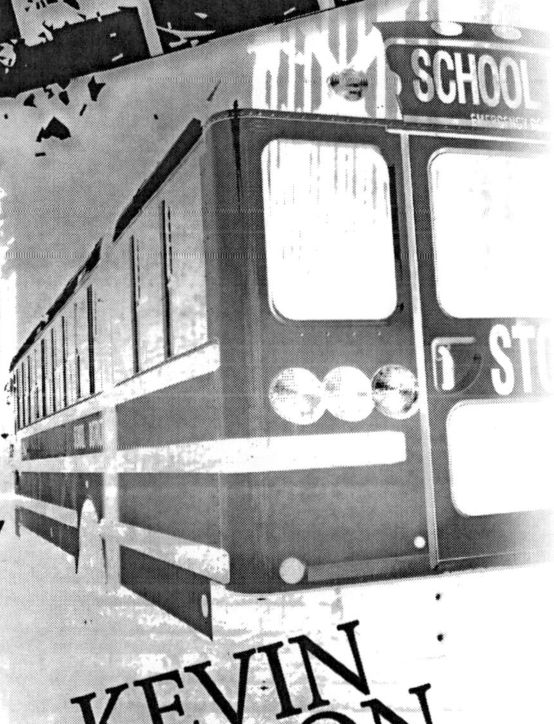

Experience the 30 Torments of Hell Firsthand Without Having to Stay for Eternity

KEVIN BENTON

LIBERTY
UNIVERSITY
Press

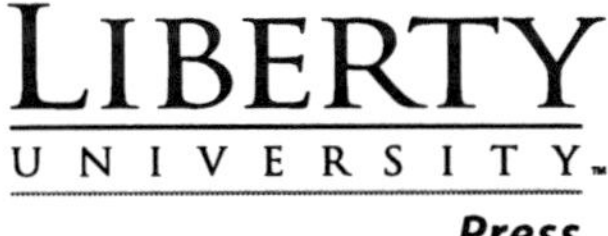

A Field Trip to Hell

by Kevin Benton

ISBN-13: 978-1-935986-05-8

Cover & Interior Design:

Megan Johnson
Johnson2Design
Johnson2Design.com

Lynchburg, VA

DEDICATION

This book is dedicated to my Lord and Savior Jesus Christ, for the personal investment he made two thousand years ago that is still in operation in my life today in spite of me.

To Deacon and Deaconess Lewis of the Mt. Zion Baptist Church in Philadelphia, who invited the kids in the neighborhood into their home for Bible Study and snacks.

To my high school coach at Mastbaum A.V.T., the late great legendary Ralph "Bones" Schneider, for seeing the Division I basketball player in me when I did not see it in myself.

To Jeff Myers, my college coach at Liberty University, for being a godly example to me and teaching our team how to use basketball as a platform from the Lord to share our faith.

To the 1993-1994 Liberty University Big South Conference Men's Basketball Championship Team.

To my oldest brother, who died at birth, Danny Benton.

To my late cousins, Ronald Harris and baby Miguel Harris.

To my late little cousin, Joseph “Boonie” Moore.

To my late Uncle Herb and Aunt Gene Adams.

To everyone who needs to be saved or wants to be sure they are saved.

To one of the greatest Christian men to ever walk the face of the earth, the late great Liberty University Chancellor, Reverend Dr. Jerry Falwell, for giving me a chance to experience a solace at Liberty University at a point in my life when I desperately needed it.

ACKNOWLEDGMENTS

God in His sovereignty and providential care has allowed some special places and people to come across my path that have helped push me closer towards my destiny. As we live out God's perfect plan for our lives, we are a sum total of the places we have been, the people we have met, and the experiences—good or bad—that accompany them. When looking through the spiritual lens of God's perspective, I understand that these places and people, and the experiences I had with them, has greatly contributed to who I am as well as the God-anointed and ordained work for such a time as this.

I would like to thank my Lord and Savior Jesus Christ for the investment he made in me two thousand years ago that is still in operation today in spite of me.

I would like to thank my beautiful and lovely wife Nikki Benton for everything.

I would like to thank my family: Minister David Benton Sr., Patricia Benton, Tamika Benton, David Benton, Jr., Heather Benton, Brianna Benton, Elder Cecil Grantham, Minister Mattie Grantham, and Jordan Grantham for all your love, encouragement, support, and prayers.

I would like to thank all of my uncles, aunts, and cousins.

I would like to thank Gerald and Ann Jordan and their family for being true and faithful friends.

I would like to thank Renew Your Mind™

I would like to thank Garry "G" Cobb, former Philadelphia Eagle and Dallas Cowboy for being available.

I would like to thank actor/comedian Sheddrick "Shed G" Garrett for all of his support.

I would like to thank actor/author and Evangelist Christopher Joy for sharing his wisdom with me.

I would like to thank my mentor and friend, Ron Baily, the host of the Trinity Broadcast Network movie, "The Lazarus Phenomenon," for speaking a word of life over me when I was in college.

I would like to thank Ms. Michal Curry, "Praise Coordinator" of the Trinity Broadcasting Network WGTW-DT 27 for believing in me and this book.

I would like to thank Reverend, Dr. Raymond M. Gordon, Senior Pastor of the St. Matthews Baptist Church in Williamstown, New Jersey, for the many years of priceless investment he made in me.

I would like to thank Pastors Dr. Clarence and Ja'Ola Walker of the Fresh Anointing Christian Center in Upper Darby, Pennsylvania, for always giving life restoring spiritual counsel from the Word of God.

I would like to thank Pastor Enoch and La Gretta Butler for their mentorship and for preaching the Word of God with power, anointing, conviction, and authority.

Acknowledgments

I would like to thank Pastor Walter and Marva Hamilton and the Christ Fellowship Church family in Herndon, Virginia, who treated me like a son of their ministry ever since I was in college.

I would like to thank the Reverend Dr. Wayne E. Croft, Sr., of the Redeemer Baptist Church in Philadelphia, Pennsylvania for an opportuniy.

I would like to thank Pastor Ralph C. Duke of the Beacon Hill Missionary Baptist Church in Herndon, Virginia for seeing my value in Christ.

I would like to thank Marquita and Marcus Collins and their family in Herndon, Virginia for being spiritual mentors to my wife and me.

I would like to thank the late Mr. George Parris and Mrs. Angie, Tracey, and Mark Parris in Sterling, Virginia, for touching my life with the love of Jesus Christ.

I would like to thank Ms. Debbie Ann Perks in the Personnel Department of the Department of Human Services for allowing God to use her as an instrument in the process of opening up a door for employment with the City of Philadelphia.

I would like to thank Ms. Andrea Corum, Account Executive and WMCN DT-44, Get It On T.V., Atlantic City, New Jersey, for supporting my book.

I would like to thank Liberty University, the world's largest Evangelical Christian university, especially the Distance Learning Program, for giving me a chance to get the best education the second time around.

I would like to thank GoodEditors.com: Leonard and Carolyn Goss, my editors.

I would like to thank Liberty University Press for being awesome and doing a great job publishing my book.

Finally, I would like to thank all of my enemies for allowing God to use them to push me closer to my destiny.

CONTENTS

PREFACE

In Christendom hell is a topic that is seldom talked about at home or especially at church. A notable and prominent survey that was taken of pastors around the country confirmed that all but a number that can literally be counted on one hand admitted to avoiding the topic due to its content and disbelief in it as a real place. In fact, the sad reality was that they only knew hell to be a place separate from God. There was a time when you would hear a sermon about hell at least once a year in church, mostly during the Easter seasons. After learning about the importance of Jesus' resurrection, one could hear about hell, allowing preachers to take advantage of the plentiful potential salvation harvest in their churches on this unique day. Whatever the reason people came to church on Easter Sunday, when so many of them did not regularly attend church, the end result was an unusual number of people making their way to the front of the church at the end of the service to dedicate or rededicate their lives to the Lord. And even though God has not given us a spirit of fear, it was the fear of going to hell that convicted many of those making these decisions.

New visitors were not the only ones benefiting from these resurrection sermons that eventually spoke on hell. Many church members who occupied the pews year in and year out never got right with God. In common parlance, they were not saved. On this day, there was something about the powerful fiery sermons on hell that brought about a change in the hearts of some longtime churchgoers. Perhaps they thought that if this place called hell is real, it would be best for them to avoid it. Who would want to go there, let alone stay for eternity? So on this extraordinary day, it was common seeing people of all ages and both genders making their way down the aisle to give their hearts and lives to Jesus Christ. The sermons on hell were so influential that even heretofore believers went down the aisle to commit themselves all over again. After all, not experiencing eternal suffering was something worth being absolutely positive about.

It must have been hard for those who were already thought to be Christians to walk down the aisle to give their hearts to Jesus, or to make sure that they were saved. The longer they sat in the pews as unbelievers while adopting the behavior of Christians, the harder it would have been to sacrifice their already projected Christian image. They would have to admit they really were not believers, and also that they had been playing the church salvation role up until this particular point. Hearing "I thought he (or she) was already a Christian" is not something anyone wants to hear when they are making a tough and sometimes scary decision to journey to the front of the church. But powerful sermons on the topic of hell had that kind of influence on many during the Easter season.

In the final analysis, the earlier one comes to God the better, but the important thing is that one does so before this life is over. More than that, any person's salvation experience at any point should be celebrated, no matter how others react or what others may think. Eternity is a long time, so any decision made for Jesus Christ is a blessing.

With the growth of church commercialism and the onset of the megachurch, which now seems to be the standard for church success, topics like sin and hell are not very popular ones for many preachers. Why is this? The graphic description of the place of torments scares off some of the membership into joining other churches that are more "user-friendly." And when they leave, they take their tithe and building fund money along with them. Filling church pews and church programs has become the priority for many large churches, rather than the spiritual condition of the people. The lives and eternal destinations of the people, both inside and outside the church, are not always the first consideration. It is true that it takes money to operate church ministries, but the souls and eternal states of men, women, boys, and girls should not be sacrificed because of it in the process.

There was a time not long ago when church success was gauged by the number of lives touched for Jesus Christ, and by the amount of people giving their souls to the Lord. Our belief was that with each soul saved, the number of residents in hell was decreased. The priority of the church was to disciple, nurture, develop, and encourage new Christians. Now it seems the success gauge has shifted to the number of people coming out to a function, and this is especially true in the so-called seeker-sensitive churches. I have noticed that numbers are so important that they are often exaggerated. The first service might have had one hundred people show up, but by the time of the second and third services, the number has been exaggerated to two hundred! The role of the church is not to count numbers but to sow seeds of Christian commitment and to inquire into the hearts and minds of worshippers while they are there.

There is nothing wrong with megachurches. Many of them were built because more space was needed, and that is a good thing. And there is nothing wrong with small storefront churches that do not need any more room. God is Sovereign, and who he chooses to bless with great or small numbers is up to him. But his priority for the lives and souls of his children and spreading the gospel of Jesus Christ throughout the world does not change, no matter what the size of the congregation. The size of a local church is important, but leading people to Christ and fulfilling the Great Commission should never be afterthoughts. Sharing the Good News is never an added-on chore, and certainly not at the expense of making sure that the church has bowling alleys, tennis courts, movie theaters, and swimming pools. These things can be used to develop the membership from a holistic development standpoint, but they must at the same time attract non-Christians in order to offer them the salvation message of Jesus Christ.

Almost everything besides sharing Christ is higher on the agendas of many churches. The church in general does not seem to have the brokenness for the lost souls that it once had. It seems the application has turned to "internal use only." In the gospel of Matthew, the Bible tells us that we are to "go therefore and make disciples of all nations" (28:19). This Scripture denotes action that lets us know we have a responsibility as Christians to get outside the church walls. A drug dealer is not likely to come to a church men's breakfast. An occupational harlot is not likely to come to a church choir concert. Yet these and everyone else need to hear the gospel message so that they can have a chance to get saved. More specifically, we witness in order to get the Word of God out into the local community, throughout the country, and ultimately throughout the world. This Scripture also lets us know that God wants his children doing his will on earth and adding to the family of God on a daily basis for his purposes and glory. The Father wants us to spend eternity in heaven with him when this life is over.

The Matthew 28:19 verse implies that it is not God's will for any person to perish. Because of the choices people will make in life, however, many people are going to perish. But Christians are not part of the problem so long as we are spreading the Word of God and making disciples of all nations. Rather, when we do our part, we are part of God's solution.

Many will remember when every Saturday morning churches all across the land handed out tracts and did door-to-door witnessing. A great percentage of the church membership participated in this evangelism, even if the pastors were not able to accompany them due to their oversight responsibilities in the church. And those who remember these Saturdays will probably also remember how the church had such a joy and zeal for the lost. We were serious about the spiritual condition of the unregenerate, and we did not want anyone going to hell. We would have witnessed to the Devil himself if we had seen him walking down the street.

The climate has changed. The "user-friendly" church's complacency and loss of focus results in people dying every day and going to hell outside of the church—and many surprisingly straight from the church pews as well. Would spiritual forefathers such as Dr. Jack Howes, Dr. Bob Gray, Chuck Misner, and well respected pastor Erwin W. Lutzer approve of pulpits not even mentioning hell? Would Christian icons like the late great Reverend Dr. Jerry Falwell, who stood on the Word of God even if he had to stand alone, be proud of the church pulpits of this era with the hell-avoiding messages? In fact Dr. Falwell was the one who staged the first Hell House in 1970, with its ghosts and ghouls, so that people might get somewhat of a visual depiction of hell and desire never to go there. Many people made decisions to get saved after seeing these presentations. Are we no longer to evangelize a dark and dying world? It is up to believers to reinstitute and rededicate themselves to bearing witness to Christ in the earth. Yes, times have changed, but that does not negate The Great Commission. Neither God nor his Word has changed, and they never will.

Our choice in the here and now influences who will choose heaven over hell in the hereafter. This challenge will be foremost in our minds as we take a field trip to hell to examine the Creator's plain warning to us all. This book is a journey through a vision of hell, the land of doubt, disbelief, and mystery, to examine what the Bible has to say about what happens when we die. We will use the Scriptures, and our sanctified imagination, along with suggestions made within the context of truth, to answer some of the most frequently asked questions pertaining to heaven and hell. And we will take a few pit stops along the way. We travel only as armchair tourists, but we will be mindful of the many that will make hell their final destination.

INTRODUCTION

Before we take our field trip to hell, let us begin by saying that everyone has their own perspective on spiritual matters. Most people feel that what they believe is the way to go and especially the way to get to God and heaven—and ultimately the way to escape hell, providing they believe in it. Perspectives differ on the things relating to the unseen spiritual realm in this life and the life to come, especially taking into consideration that there are at least forty thousand different religions in the world, not counting all those who do not claim any particular faith at all. The last thing I want to do is turn anyone away from the message of the Bible by seeming critical, judgmental, or dogmatic about my theological stance—despite the fact that I am not an advocating devotee of the spiritual uniformity myth. Instead, I want my approach to be like that of a mailman delivering a gift of the Gift Giver to the world, while at the same time desiring not to be hypocritical in the very same area I am challenging believers pertaining to their evangelistic responsibility. This gift can not only change one's eternal destination as it pertains to heaven and hell, but it can change one's life right here in the present. That is why I want to challenge my readers in love according to my strong personal beliefs and convictions. I will use the Scripture to support the facts, but once in a while I will even refer to educational, scientific, and practical evidences to support the truths presented in this book. I will also use everyday situations and circumstances to help solidify some of my arguments. Yet it all boils down to what the individual chooses to do with the gift from the Gift Giver.

I have come to my point of view on this topic by studying what Scripture has to say. I consider Scripture a revelation not only to me, but to all, and by sharing it with others they can weigh their own spiritual state. The Bible commands us as Christians to "go therefore and make disciples of all nations, baptizing them in the name of the Father and of the Son and of the Holy Spirit. Teaching them to observe all things that I have commanded you; and lo, I am with you always, even to the end of the age" (Matt. 28:19-20).

I want to begin by presenting some food for thought as we get ready to move forward on our journey together to consider the afterlife. My logical process goes like this: If hell is real and salvation is the requirement to escape hell, and if the Bible is true, and if one person is a believer and the other is not, then the believer comes out on top. On the other hand, if salvation is not the requirement to escape hell, providing that hell is real, both the believer and the unbeliever lose. But it does seem interesting to me that in these two cases the unbeliever loses twice.

As a child, I remember coming home from school one day. Being the first in the house, I would always eat an afternoon snack (a peanut butter and jelly sandwich and a glass of milk), change my clothes, and finish my homework before my mom came home. After completing all of my school assignments, I would grab a pillow and a blanket, lay on the floor in the front room with all the lights out, and turn on my favorite cat and mouse cartoon, *Tom & Jerry.*

On this particular day they showed the episode when Tom, while chasing Jerry as he does every episode, gets run over by a piano that came rolling down the steps. Tom gets crushed by the piano and dies. He has an out-of-body experience were his soul leaves his body and gets on an escalator that goes to heaven. When his soul finally arrives at the pearly gates to see if God will let him into heaven, he looks at all the deeds that Tom has done throughout his life. He sees that Tom has treated Jerry very badly and must make amends in order to be able to get into heaven. God handed Tom a piece of paper and told him he had twenty four hours to get Jerry's signature on it. After that, Tom could spend eternity in heaven. God told him if he was not able to get the signature that he would be sent to hell.

The scene then switched to hell, which was depicted as a very dark valley full of fire and brimstone. Spike the bulldog, portraying the Devil, was red and had horns on his head, a long red tail, a red cape, and a pitchfork in his hand. Looking upward, after God instructed Tom of the consequences of not getting Jerry's signature, Spike began talking and laughing with a sinister voice and saying, "Send him to me, send him down, send him down."

At this moment, being home alone with all the lights out, except for the light coming from the TV screen, I got very scared. I became so afraid that I could not watch the rest of the episode. I covered myself with my blanket and hid under the covers as I listened to the rest of the story. I did not move until my mom came home from work.

As a child I heard about heaven and hell in church, but this cartoon was the first time in my life I saw a visual depiction of hell. Being a child, and even though it was a cartoon, this was very frightening. That episode changed my life. I learned the importance of being very careful how I treated people on a daily basis. Most importantly, even in my childlike thinking, I knew from that point on that if hell was a real place, I never wanted to go there.

I remember my mother taking my brother and me to church as children. We sat in the congregation listening to many sermons about heaven. I did not want to die at that moment in order to see if what I was hearing was true, but I was deeply encouraged. The reason was that I believed in the salvation message of the finished work of Jesus Christ's death on the cross for the sins of humankind. And that message was clear about Christians going to heaven. We were going to heaven because Jesus hung on the cross, was buried, and rose on the third day with all power in his hands. It is because of the resurrection of the Savior that we know Jesus Christ is real and that we can have hope in the life to come. The apostle Paul challenges us about the real hope we have in Christ:

> *Now if Christ is preached that He has been raised from the dead, how do some among you say that there is no resurrection of the dead? But if there is no resurrection of the dead, then*

> *Christ is not risen. And if Christ is not risen, then our preaching is empty and your faith is also empty. Yes, and we are found false witnesses of God, because we have testified of God that He raised up Christ, whom He did not raise up—if in fact the dead do not raise. For if the dead do not raise, then Christ is not risen. And if Christ is not risen, your faith is futile; you are still in your sins! Then also those who have fallen asleep in Christ have perished. If in this life only we have hope in Christ, we are of all men the most pitiable (1 Corinthians 15:12-19).*

Paul clearly states that if Christ did not rise from the dead, then we have no hope in this life or in the life to come. The consequence of that is that we are still in our sins and still in need of a Savior. But the Good News is that Christ returned from the dead, just as he said he would, and that Christians will spend eternity in heaven.

I also remember attending church and hearing sermons about the significance of Christ's resurrection that eventually dealt with hell at least once a year during Easter time. The effect it had on me was to send me down the aisle seeking salvation during the altar call time after time. I kept doing this until I gained more understanding about the security of my salvation. Until then, the messages on hell scared me into getting saved every year, and somehow the part about burning in the flames for eternity gave me the courage to get up out of my pew. Those Easter sermons that got around to the hell message emphasized that God was a God of love, but he was also a jealous God of wrath who could and did send people to hell. He was not a God to be played with and was to be reverently feared and respected. Even after hearing sermons about hell and making what I thought was the easy choice of picking heaven over it, I still had many questions about this eternal place of horrifying torments, and I wanted to know what it was really like. In the meantime, the immediate sources of information that helped me learn what hell was like to a great degree were the sermons in church. Watching Christian-based movies depicting hell, and my neighborhood outdoor tent drama ministry during the summer time, also contributed to making hell a reality for me. All of these vehicles served to answer some of the many questions I had about hell as they painted a vivid picture that allowed me to see for myself. The best thing about learning this way was that I could seemingly experience hell without having to really go or stay for eternity. The hardest part for me at the time (which is really the easiest part) was taking God at his word and believing it was true.

In general, people have always been intrigued by the vast unanswered questions about the afterlife especially as it pertains to an unseen God, heaven, and hell. With all the various religions that exist in today's world, people try to connect with God in their own way, and they have been doing this ever since the beginning of time. The reason is so that some closure can be brought to these seemingly unanswerable questions that lead to a benevolent afterlife. This intrigue has even led to a number of Hollywood movies portraying heaven as a beautiful place in the sky for the good people whose good deeds outweigh their bad deeds. Hell, on the other hand, is portrayed as a fiery underground place of torments and punishments for the bad or evil people whose bad deeds outweigh their good deeds. According to the Bible, Hollywood got only some of this right. In the gospel of Matthew, we read, "Now behold, one came to Him, 'Good Teacher, what good thing shall I do that I may have eternal life?' So He said to him, 'Why do you call Me good? No one is good but One, that is God. But if you want to enter into life, keep the commandments'" (19:16-17).

This Scripture lets us know that doing good deeds cannot help one enter heaven, and that doing bad deeds does not necessarily rule out heaven for anyone because "no one is good." God's will is that we do good to all, especially those of the household of faith. However, from God's perspective, it is not what we do but rather what we are that determines whether we are good or bad. If one does not want to wait until they die to find out what their final destination might be, I suggest reading a very vivid picture of heaven in the New Testament's book of Revelation, chapters twenty-one and twenty-two. There is also a graphic depiction of hell in the gospel of Luke, chapter sixteen, regarding the story of Lazarus and the rich man.

Many people—and this includes believers—ponder deep down in their hearts whether hell is a real place. Maybe if somehow people could get some concrete physical evidence, that attitude would change. Or, as absurd as it may sound, talk to someone who has been there who could describe what it was like and prove it really does exist.

People might not be honest enough to admit it to anyone, but they would be in favor of it. Especially for those who would be classified as the doubting Thomas types who will not believe unless they see, touch, and hear for themselves in order to be convinced. We would not even mind visiting hell just as long as we were given the assurance up front of not having to experience any pain or torments down there. Even scientific research proves that people enjoy the feeling of being afraid, so long as it is under controlled circumstances. We would want this security, in our minds, just in case this place really is all that has been said about it.

There are those who have written about out-of-body experiences when they travelled to heaven or hell. One author explained why God had him visit hell. He said he experienced this trip because "my own people don't even believe that hell is real." A well respected man named Doctor Rawlings, who was a former devout atheist, now a born again believer, was quoted as saying that he considered all religion, "Hocus-pocus and death—nothing more than a painless extinction." Until one day something happened in his life that changed him forever and he gave his life to Jesus. He was trying to resuscitate a man who was terrified and screaming and who was going in and out of an out-of-body experience. The dying man said he was descending into the flames of hell. The doctor was quoted in his book as saying:

Each time he regained a heartbeat and respiration, the patient screamed, "I am in Hell!" He was terrified and pleaded with me to help him. I

> *was scared to death and then I noticed a genuinely alarmed look on his face. He had a terrified look worse than the expression seen in death. This patient had a grotesque grimace expressing sheer horror! His pupils were dilated, and he was perspiring and trembling. He looked as if his hair was "on end." Then still another strange thing happened. He said, "Don't you understand I am in hell? Don't let me go back to hell!" The man was serious and it finally occurred to me that he was indeed in trouble. He was in a panic like I had never seen before. No one who could have heard his screams and saw the look of terror on his face could doubt for a single minute that he was actually in a place called hell!*

On a more personal note, I remember talking to one of my teammates that I used to play basketball with at my former church. Having left that church some years before, the Lord laid it on my heart to call him as I was scrolling through some numbers of an old cell phone that I found while cleaning out some drawers in my kitchen. Upon talking to my friend that day he told me that he had recently been in a serious car accident and almost died because the car flipped over a few times. The car was totaled. I told him it was a miracle and that he was blessed to still be alive. He agreed and then told me that while he was unconscious after the accident, he began feeling his feet and legs burning in excruciating pain, and that he began to scream. He then said when he regained consciousness he woke up on a hospital bed. Understanding what that meant, I asked for his permission to pray the sinner's prayer with him. He agreed, repeated the sinner's prayer after me, and came to faith in Christ right then and there.

If the world has desired physical witness and proof of hell, it has already received it. For some, this type of experience brings assurance that the afterlife is authentic. Because of the alarming characteristics of dreams, even scientists who have done studies on dreams are now admitting that these out-of-body experiences and testimonies about visitations to hell are real. According to them, dreams tend to be segmented, and most of them are forgotten. On the other hand, recollections of these testimonials are organized and processional and the people who share these dreams share visions that are remarkably similar. These accounts solidify their current belief systems and soothe their hushed, inward disbelief.

One main problem with accepting the concept of hell is the difficulty in understanding why a loving God would send anyone to hell in the first place. What is hell really like? Do souls experience literal fire and brimstone, as has sometimes been described? Is it possible that one could burn and suffer everlasting conscious torment? Would serious believers of another religion be sent to hell because they are not Christians? Does what we believe really determine if we go to hell when life is over? Is Jesus Christ just as real and alive today as he was yesterday? These questions and others cause many to doubt the implications of a literal hell. In this book I will look to Scripture to support the existence of both heaven and hell. If God is not real and his Word is not true, then our faith is in vain, there is probably no heaven or hell, and we are of all men most pitiable.

The first time hell is mentioned in the Bible is in the book of Numbers, when God judged Korah, Dathan, Abiram, their families, and the two hundred and fifty men who followed them. They are sent to hell for their wickedness.

> *Now it came to pass, as he (Moses) finished speaking all these words, that the ground split apart under them, and the earth opened up its mouth and swallowed them up, with their households and all the men with Korah, with all their goods. So they and all those with them went down alive into the pit; the earth closed over them, and they perished from among the assembly. Then all Israel who were around them fled at their cry, for they said, "Lest the earth swallow us up also!" And fire came out from the Lord and consumed the two hundred and fifty men who were offering incense (16:31-35).*

This Old Testament Scripture tells us four things right away. First, hell is a real place with real torments. In fact, as we will see later, there are at least thirty different types of torments going on simultaneously and the fire is not the worst aspect. To add to this, hell, being the ultimate place of suffering and a vast unsolved mystery, more than likely has more torments that have not been revealed. Second, while people may feel they have gone through "hell on earth," this

Scripture gives us some clarity about the location of hell actually not being on the earth. Third, the God who is known for his love has another side that needs to be respected, for the opening of the earth shows the wrath God is capable of. Four, when considering the number of people who fell down into the pit at one time, this Scripture informs us there will be many people in hell. It is even possible that more people will be consigned to hell than to heaven. The gospel of Matthew confirms this: "Enter by the narrow gate; for wide is the gate and broad is the way that leads to destruction, and there are many who go in by it. Because narrow is the gate and difficult is the way which leads to life, and there are few who find it" (7:13-14).

My presupposition is that hell is a real place, and there are real people there. My purpose in writing *A Field Trip to Hell* is eightfold: I want, first, to explore with my readers whether there is a divine saving grace and knowledge, and if the evidence shows we will be spending eternity in either heaven or hell. My second purpose is to challenge professing Christians to make sure they understand the ramifications of true faith and the afterlife. Even "professing Christians" can wind up in a real place of punishment called hell. The third purpose is to motivate believers to develop a passion about fulfilling the Great Commission. Fourth, I want to take readers on a field trip to hell by way of the Word of God incorporated into a story. I am hoping our trip will bring some understanding and clarity to the most frequently asked questions about the dreadful nature of hell while proposing some nontraditional aspects. The fifth purpose of this book is to encourage those without faith to come to faith. The sixth purpose is to encourage believers to make sure their questions on the afterlife are answered. The seventh purpose of this book is to hearten those who have made decisions for Jesus Christ. To that end, there is a short prayer at the end of this book. And the eighth purpose of this book is to offer some essential instructions for growth in the Christian life.

For now, in the first three chapters, I want to tell you a little bit about my path and what gave birth to this book. It is a journey that entails blessings and triumph, sin and disobedience, but ultimately purpose and destiny that came by way of a personal visitation to hell. Then, just before we begin our field trip to hell, we will answer some of the most frequently asked theological questions pertaining to God and hell.

CHAPTER ONE

A New Beginning: Off to a Good Brand New Start

During the summer after my junior year in high school, I was prompted by the Holy Spirit and the pastor during an altar call. I went up to the front of the church to rededicate my life to the Lord. I had been a believer since I was eleven years old, but in rededicating my life I decided I wanted to get baptized as well. Getting baptized was one of the greatest experiences of my life. After being immersed in the water and bought back up, I did not feel the same as I did before. I felt a sense of peace, and it seemed like heavy weights had been lifted off my shoulders. I also felt a sense of holiness and purity, as it truly seemed that God had wiped my sinful slate clean and I was truly starting over again. This blessing of favor had nothing to do with the water; it came from my willingness to be obedient to God's Word. Mostly I felt secure in the fact that God was pleased with me and was smiling down on this monumental moment in my life. I was off to a good brand new start. Afterward, I felt a new lease on life, with a joy, a glow, and a zeal that permeated me as I could sense the favor and presence of God in my life.

I played varsity basketball for Mastbaum High School in Philadelphia in the Public League. My sophomore and junior years went well as I earned Fifth Team All-Public and then Second Team All-Public respectively. However, after rededicating my life to the Lord, this sense of closeness with God carried over into my senior year at Mastbaum. Though not without its ups and downs, my senior year was one where everything seemed to go right and eventually fell into place. It appeared that everything I got involved in was blessed, and I prospered on and off the court. That year I averaged about thirty points a game with an average of fourteen rebounds. I became Mastbaum's second all time leading scorer with 1,289 career points—behind girls varsity basketball player Jennifer Ricco, who amassed 1,442 points. I was the number one male all-time leading scorer in school history, and the *Philadelphia Daily News* voted me the third best player in school history. Some other credible basketball sources considered me to be arguably the best basketball player in the school's history, but at any rate it was an honor to be considered one of the best. That season we earned a twenty-nine and nine record, which made us the ninth best team in the city at the time. During my sophomore and junior years our team did not even make the playoffs, with a five and seventeen and a ten and twelve record respectively.

My team lost my brother David to graduation, so during my senior year the leadership responsibility fell to me. I led us through the regular season and into the second round of the playoffs against nationally ranked powerhouse Simon Gratz High School. Gratz starred the likes of Rasheed Wallace, a former NBA champion, and Aaron McKie, a former Philadelphia 76er, two of my good friends I might add. We had just beaten Kareem Townes, South Philadelphia High School All-American and LaSalle University star, in overtime in the first round of the playoffs. I scored thirty-six points and grabbed fourteen rebounds in a comeback win to help us advance to the quarterfinals to play against Simon Gratz. During this monumental win, we were down twenty points late in the game and our fans began leaving Southern's gym assuming we lost the game. When they read the papers the next day in school, they could not believe it. The *Philadelphia Inquirer* headlines read "Mastbaum tops Southern in O.T. behind Benton's 36." This win was significant because Southern beat us in the regular season by seventeen points at their place, and Kareem Townes scored a game high thirty-four points. After the game was over, I got a call from Jonathan Haines, former Germantown Friends High and Villanova Wild Cats star, and Aaron McKie, of Simon Gratz High. Jonathan asked me how the game went, and I told him that we won in overtime. He then asked me how many points I scored, even though I knew he already had the answer. I just humbly said, "I had thirty-six points, that's all." Jonathan then said, "You know who y'all play next, right?" I said, "Yeah man, Simon Gratz." Aaron McKie, said, "Y'all better lace them up tight and y'all better be ready." Jonathan and Aaron continued talking trash, and I just listened and laughed because it was all in fun and the competitive spirit. We said we would see one another next week at the game.

To make a long story short, we lost by seventeen points to Simon Gratz. I faced double and triple teams and did not play as well as I could have, even though I left everything out there on the floor. With legendary coaches like John Chaney looking on, I picked a bad time to have my only bad game of the season. Other coaches from around the area, and especially the Philadelphia area "big five" schools, watched as Simon Gratz dismantled us. I was exhausted and spent, but, as I told Ted Silary, the legendary *Philadelphia Daily News* high school basketball sports writer, I was just glad that it was over. Shortly after that I turned my focus to the Public League All-Star game, where I would of course see some of my Simon Gratz rivals again.

1990 Philadelphia Public League Player of the Year

At the end of the season I received the most prestigious award a Philadelphia Public League high school basketball player could be given—the 1990 "Philadelphia Public League Player of the Year." It was such a blessing to be selected for such a great honor, when there were other players who could have easily been selected. Our senior class was touted as one of the best in Philadelphia High School basketball history. Our senior class was so good that the Sonny Hill league took the top seniors in the city and put us in the college league. We won the championship in that league as well. Being given the player of the year award in front of my legendary coach, the late great Ralph "Bones" Schneider, my teammates, and basketball players from around the city was a blessing. Legend and Hall of Famer Sonny Hill himself, whose league I grew up in and developed as a basketball player, came out to support me personally. His staff also came along with him, including the legendary college and pro talent scout and pro workout specialist, the late great John Hardnett. This was an experience I will never forget as long as I live.

When I received these awards, my mother was very sick at the time and in the hospital. My mom and dad did not let me know how serious her condition was, but I now know she could have died without having a rare emergency surgery to stop internal hemorrhaging. My mom would always send messages through my dad to encourage me because he came to all of my brother's and my games. My brother and I played together at Mastbaum for two years. He was one year ahead of me in school. Of course when I had the opportunity to speak at the podium after receiving this prestigious award, I thanked my brother, but I had to give all praise to my Lord and Savior Jesus Christ (which was not a very popular thing to do at the time). I knew that I was given a platform, because when you are the "player of the year" who dismantled all the competition, people tend to listen to what you say and respect you. I also gave credit to the legendary Public League champion Simon Gratz, along with coaching great Bill Ellerbee, Aaron McKie, Harry Moore, Rasheed Wallace, and the entire Simon Gratz basketball team.

Garbage Kev

I had come a long way from my humble beginnings going over to Johnson's playground in southwest Philadelphia to play basketball. No one would pick me for their team, and I kept on getting pushed back until the lights went out and it was too late to play anymore. I remember during little league games the fans nicknamed me "garbage Kev" and they made fun of me—the tall, skinny, uncoordinated kid wearing Bo-Bo's (an unnamed brand) sneakers.

When I played in leagues at Kingsessing playground also in southwest Philadelphia, people who did not even know me called me names from the stands with my mom and dad sitting right there. My dad would turn around and say, "Hey, that's my son," and get into arguments from time to time. The constant rejection I received and felt as a little leaguer up to and throughout my freshman year in high school hurt very badly, and it made me angry inside.

To add to all this, after my freshman year at Overbrook High School, around the time when I was in the process of transferring to Mastbaum so that I could play with my brother David who was already playing varsity, I overheard my mother praying downstairs one day. I was listening at the top of the steps as I heard her crying and talking to someone. I realized that she was downstairs by herself, talking to God. The prayer I heard her pray made me want to take basketball a lot more seriously. She said, "Lord I don't have the money to send my kids to college, and I pray you would bless them so that they won't ever have to beg from anyone. Even if I have to go into debt for the rest of my life, God, my kids are going to college." She ended her prayer with two verses from the Psalms: "I have been young, and now am old; Yet I have not seen the righteous forsaken, Nor his descendants begging bread. He is ever merciful, and lends; And his descendants are blessed" (37:25-26).

Even to this very day God has been true to his Word. As a result of hearing my mother's prayer I started getting up at 6:00 AM to practice, practice, and practice basketball every day. When I got to Johnson's playground, Randy

Woods, former LaSalle star and former Los Angeles Clipper, would already be there working hard on his game. Randy would be down one end of the court, and I would be down the other. After practice at Johnson's, I walked sixteen blocks to Drexel University in Center City Philadelphia, from 49th and Greenway where I used to live, to practice some more. I hid out for a while from the other kids in my neighborhood, just to dedicate myself to practicing every day, twice a day. This was the summer I grew four inches, from 6 feet to 6 feet, four inches.

Four Extra Inches

Towards the end of that summer I went to Mastbaum High School's coach Ralph "Bones" Schneider's summer basketball camp, where my brother David was one of the varsity players and counselors. The camp was held up in the mountains, and I loved getting out of the city for a change. I had had a tough basketball experience at Overbrook my freshman year and I was already in the process of transferring to Mastbaum so I could play basketball with my brother, one of the best point guards in Philadelphia Public League history. It was a perfect fit. Dave was the starting point guard, and I was the swing man. Since he was my brother I knew I would get the ball. We even had our own signals and plays that we orchestrated within the coach's system. We had a lot of fun at basketball camp. Going into my sophomore year, I transferred from Overbrook to Mastbaum, and when the season started in November all the practicing I did came in handy. The extra four inches I grew didn't hurt, either. I was the tallest guy on the team and could jump the highest. I went out during the tryouts and made the team, even earning a starting position. By the end of the season I averaged fifteen points and ten rebounds each game, and I was selected Fifth Team All-Public by the *Philadelphia Daily News.*

The following year as a junior I was selected to the Second Team All-Public, and I just kept getting better and better. My brother had already graduated by the time I became a senior, and he had gone on to play in college. I was selected to the First Team All-Public, First Team All-City, First Team All-State, and the "Philadelphia Public League Player of the Year." I was unstoppable. My brother and I returned to the playgrounds each summer after my sophomore year to wreak havoc on the court. We won so many championships over the course of our high school years that we had to throw away all of our trophies because we had no place to store them. I do wish we could have won a high school championship together, but the power houses during that time were Frankford High and Simon Gratz. Still, I was on my way.

After my senior year basketball season was over, I was invited to play in many post season all-star games. According to NCAA guidelines, however, we were only allowed to play in two. I chose to play in the Public League All-Star game where for the last time in high school I had to face my good friends Aaron McKie and Harry Moore from Simon Gratz. Aaron and I actually guarded each other during the game, and while I scored twenty points, he only had two. I must admit I had a little extra motivation due to the fact that Simon Gratz beat us convincingly during the last game of my high school career.

The man who coached my team in the Public League All-Star game was Mr. Beckett, my ninth grade junior varsity coach at Overbrook High School in West Philadelphia. I had had a bad basketball experience there. I was only thirteen years old, going on fourteen, and I was already six feet tall. The reason I went to Overbrook in the first place was because of their art magnet program, which was the best in the city. My late Uncle Herb Adams, who coached Randy Woods and me during little leagues, told me he would talk to the varsity coach, Mark Lavin, to get me on the varsity team. I did not expect to get a lot of playing time, and I certainly did not expect to start, but I felt I was good enough to at least make the team. Even though I did pretty well during the tryouts, Coach Lavin thought I was too young for the varsity squad, so he sent me down to the junior varsity team. I actually started JV until Coach Beckett checked all the player's records to see how our grades were. When he checked mine, he found out I was only thirteen at the time. He sat me down and told me he was not able to start me because the other guys were fourteen, fifteen, and sixteen years old. Not only could I not play varsity ball, but now I could not even play junior varsity. This hurt very badly because it was not due to someone else being better than me, but because of my age. So I just sat watching the games from the bench game in and game out. Sometimes I got in for two minutes at the end of the game (what they call "garbage time") when our team was winning by twenty-five or thirty points. That lasted until the second report cards came around.

When the second round of report cards was issued, just about all of the coach's top players, who were the older guys, did not make the grades and had to be cut from the team. This meant I not only got the chance to play, but I got the chance to start. I took advantage of the opportunity (with a little chip on my shoulder) and ended up leading the team in scoring with twelve points a game to become our leading scorer for the remainder of the season. When that year was over I went to Mastbaum's summer basketball camp before transferring there for my sophomore year. I played on the team with my brother, and after our high school careers we were selected by the *Philadelphia Daily News* as the third best brother combination in Philadelphia Public League history at that time, behind Troy and Andre Daniels, former Lamberton High and Drexel University stars, and Jason and Carlin Warley, former Frankford High and St. Joseph's University stars.

More All-Star Games

The coach who had rejected me because of my age in ninth grade was now coaching me as the top senior in the Public League All-Star game. In the locker room before the game he said, "I told them you were going to be special. I told them you were going to be good." My mother nicknamed me "Special K" when I was a baby, because I survived being born three months premature and the nurses told my mother that I was going to be a special child. But Coach

Beckett did not know that. I was not angry or bitter at him, and I knew it was not a coincidence that he was coaching me on that kind of platform. God brought things full circle to show that you need to be very careful who you talk about, look down upon, or laugh at, because they might be a child of God. Now, every time they have a Public League All-Star game, they list the leading scorers of each of the games in the program, dating back to the first year the game was played leading all the way up to the present day. To go back to watch the All-Star games years and years later, and to still see my name in the history books as the leading scorer in 1990 sometimes makes me a little emotional. It vindicated me from my ninth grade year at Overbrook while playing JV and it also showed that God had his hand on me and was working in my life.

I also played in the USA versus Colorado All-Star game on Saturday, April 7, 1990, as I was selected a "Joint Effort All-American." Some of my teammates included Raphael "Rap" Curry, former Penn Wood High and St. Joseph's University star, and Matt Maloney, former University of Pennsylvania star and Houston Rocket. "Rap" Curry and I are now very active in our individual local churches, and it is so funny to see life come full circle again for us. The USA team was a great experience because on top of playing, I was selected to participate in the slam dunk contest the day before the actual all-star game. It was like the NBA's All-Star weekend. I could do any dunk Dominique Wilkins could do. Dominique is a nine-time NBA All-Star and former player with the Atlanta Hawks. He was nicknamed "The Human Highlight Film," and he was my idol.

I even went out and got a high top faded S-Curl, just like him. I came in second place because I missed a few difficult dunks I normally would have made but it was a lot of fun.

This was when I had the opportunity to meet Lisa Leslie, former WNBA's Los Angeles Sparks star, who played for the USA's girl's team. The high light of the slam dunk contest was when Lisa, who was 6' 5" tall, went up with one hand leaning sideways a little and dunked it. The crowd went off, including me. She was out there competing with the guys and holding her own. She did not do any complicated dunks, but the fact remained that she was a young lady out there with guys and dunking it. The next day, during the All-Star game, I played very well and scored fifteen points and grabbed eleven rebounds as the University of Delaware's head coach looked on. I saw him sitting in the stands, and after the game he made his presence known as he walked by me. He was not able to say anything to me at that time, due to NCAA recruiting guidelines and stipulations. It was an awesome experience.

Red-Letter Day

One month later I received a treasured piece of correspondence in the mail when I got my SAT results on Saturday, April 29, 1990, at around 4:00 PM. It was a red-letter day for me because I had scored high enough on my SAT test to be eligible to play my freshman year, and not have to sit out due to the NCAA proposition 48 guidelines. The guidelines stated at that time if a student athlete did not score a minimum of 700 on the SAT, they had to sit out their first year of college athletically and forfeit that year of eligibility towards their athletic scholarship. Since then the NCAA's SAT requirement for student athletes has been moved up in order to be eligible to play their freshman year.

I remember that day just like it was yesterday. It was a Saturday morning, and I was watching TV in the living room as I waited for the mail. I left the screen door locked, but the front door was open. The mail normally came around 3:00 PM, but today it came a little late. One of my good friends, John Battle, was the mailman. John and I grew up together playing pick-up basketball games at Johnson's playground. I heard our gate open and got up to run to the door. John looked through his stack and found the letter I had been waiting for, the results of which would determine my future. If the SAT score was in my favor, that would put my dream of playing Division 1 basketball in motion. The letter seemed to glow, but I had peace in my heart because I had taken some SAT prep courses with Mike and Elaine Brenner. The Brenner's directed an SAT-preparation business in Norristown, Pennsylvania. The interesting thing was that I had the chance to play against the basketball team they sponsored, called M & E Trucks, when I was twelve years old in the Media, Pennsylvania, basketball league. My Uncle Herb used to take us on his little league travel team to play outside the city to teach us how to play in environments we were not accustomed to or comfortable playing in. He did this in order to help us to become better basketball players. To see life come full circle once again was definitely the hand of the Lord.

My mom and dad taught me to treat people with respect when you come in contact with them because you never know when you are going to come in contact with them again later on in life. Since I had always showed Mr. Brenner and his team respect and good sportsmanship, he helped me with my SAT preparation. Nonetheless, I opened my letter and all I did was look at the beginning of the first number, which was a 4, and the beginning of the second number, which was a 3, and I just yelled, "I got it, I got it, I passed the test!" After having scored 680 twice, and dipping to 640, I had passed the test with a score of 740. I know that this score is nothing to brag about. Even though I got good grades in school, I never imagined I was a whiz kid. I was typically an A, B, and a few Cs type of student. All I wanted to do was to go to college and play basketball for a Division 1 program so my mom and dad would not have to go into debt paying for my education. That day I could not help but think back two years prior to the day I heard her prayer while listening at the top of the steps. This made the moment even more special because God had answered her prayer not only for me but for my brother as well. My family rejoiced with me, and it was a very happy and exciting time for us. We contacted the University of Delaware and set up a meeting to sign my letter of intent, giving me a full scholarship to the university. We later contacted Ted Silary of the *Philadelphia Daily News* and he did a write up in the paper with the headlines reading, "Red-letter day for Benton, passes 700, will play at Delaware." This was a dream come true.

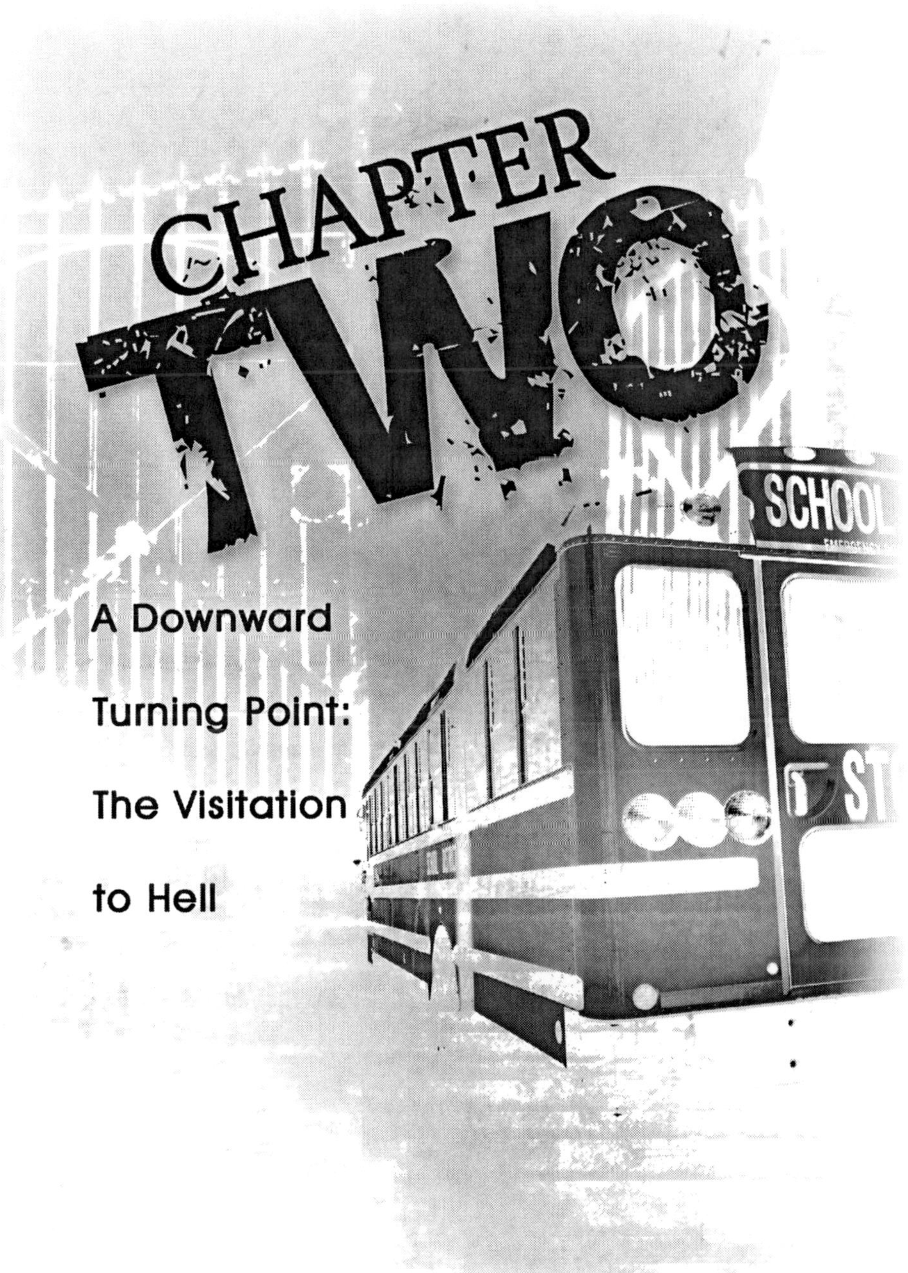

CHAPTER TWO

A Downward Turning Point: The Visitation to Hell

Things began taking a turn for the worse because I began having relationship problems with my girlfriend of a year. This was bad timing with all of the excitement surrounding how my senior year had just ended. I met her at a summer pre-college preparation program at Villanova University. The program was designed to prepare us for college work and college life. It was great because during the course of the program we were considered Villanova students and had our ID (that we were so proud of). We had access to facilities like the swimming pool and the weight room. Of course I had to make my way to the gym where the Villanova team played. The basketball team was running inner squad scrimmages. I met Doug West, one of my idols and a former NBA player. I also met seven foot center Tom Griese, Harold Jensen, Garey Masey, and the entire Villanova team. I was in heaven and in awe at the same time because these were guys I watched on television.

I was only a junior in high school at the time, coming off of a Second-Team All-City year, but one of the players asked me to play. The highlight of the game for me was when I faced Garey Masey at the top of the key just having come off a screen from the left wing. I gave a fake left that he went for, drove to the right, and went straight down the lane. I took off with two feet from the dotted line with two hands on the ball, pulled the ball behind my head, and dunked it really, really hard on him. The people in the gym wondered who I was and stared at me as I ran back on defense. Garey Masey came down court the very next play, took me in the post, backed me down, and turned and dunked the ball right in my face. I knew I could have played at Villanova, but surprisingly, they did not recruit me. I heard that Rollie Massamino, the coach of the Villanova Wildcats at that time, was not very interested in city public league players because of some of the stereotypes that were attached to Philly basketball players. The truth was, he was right. Some players tended to give us a bad name. I wish he had given me a chance, because I did not fit the stereotype of the typical Philadelphia basketball player on or off the court.

Some of my classmates in the pre-college preparation program saw me play with the team, including a young lady who sat in front of me and appeared to be very nice. We began speaking to each other more and more. One day after class we talked and expressed our interest in one another as it pertains to dating. I told her I would like to date her under some conditions. I told her I was a virgin and planned to stay that way until I got married. I also told her that I wanted to marry a virgin. I believed in courtship more than just dating because I did not want to waste my time with the break-up and make-up drama that goes on in more casual relationships. I was not trying to judge her if she was not a virgin, but I did not want pre-marital sex to be an issue in our relationship. I just felt that if I was preserving myself, I had the right to choose someone who was doing the same thing. I wanted to put everything on the table before we considered ourselves a couple. She told me she was virgin as well and that she shared my same morals and values.

Things started getting dicier in our relationship towards the end of my senior year when my girlfriend dropped a bomb on me. She told me on Valentine's Day, eight months into our relationship, that she had something to tell me. At this time I really cared about her, so I was scared about what the news would be. She told me I was frustrating her because she really was not a virgin and that she wanted to have sex with me. I felt like I had a knot in my throat and was shocked. I began asking questions, some of which she did not want to answer, and I just cried. I told her that that was not fair, and that if she had told me the truth when I asked her eight months before, I would have never dated her—no matter how good looking she was. We went through the after effects of this dilemma for about five months. I wish that I would have had the courage to break off the relationship, but I did not. Along with her pressuring me and fearing that she would leave me, I just stayed. On top of all this, I was concerned because she was already headed to the University of Delaware when the officials there pulled some strings to help her get into the school because they wanted me playing there. All these things converged, and eventually I started having sex with her. I know I still had a choice, and I take full responsibility for myself and my sin, but I felt trapped.

Second Virginity

I will admit I was always curious about sex but because I had never experienced it up until that point, I did not know what I was missing. Therefore, I did not miss it. When it was over, I felt guilty, dirty, unclean, and a little angry. I had waited all those years and a few more would not have hurt me until I got married. I was not a virgin anymore, and I could never regain my innocence. I felt I had let God down. Afterwards, my girlfriend and I talked about it, and we repented, agreed to break off the relationship, and made a decision that we were not going to have sex again until we got married to whoever we would marry. I had my concerns about how it would be with both of us on the same campus and not being an item, but we both knew that our behavior would have continued if we did not take these steps.

Another thing went wrong when I arrived at the University of Delaware campus in the fall of my freshman year. The top assistant coach who recruited me, Dennis Felton, was leaving Delaware to go to Tulane University. One of the things he told my dad and me was, "If things don't work out here, you can always come to Tulane." This statement did not seem right to us, especially coming from a nice man such as Coach Felton. He was the reason I decided to go to UD, and I appreciated how he showed genuine concern for me and especially my mother when she was sick while I was in high school. I would later find out that without Coach Felton there, I would end up on an island by myself with no one to be a voice for me on the coaching staff. I just wish he would have told us ahead of time that he was leaving, because that definitely would have influenced my coming in the first place, let alone staying after he left.

At any rate, in spite of my backsliding, I had just lived through one of the best years of my life, from rededicating my life to the Lord and getting baptized, leading all the way up to earning a scholarship to play basketball at Delaware. I could not imagine anything going sour at this point, so I stayed at Delaware and waited for the carryover from the blessing from my senior year in high school. After repenting and making a decision to abstain again, I got what preachers classify as my second virginity. Gaining some momentum over time, I got back the very same glow and zeal that I had after I got baptized. In fact, after turning my life around and focusing on all the blessings I just experienced in high school, my zeal for the Lord had increased. I was on fire again because I knew it was only God who had blessed me the way he did that year. All I wanted to do was read the Bible during my spare time and witness to my teammates about the goodness of the Lord. I was bold for Christ and not ashamed of the gospel. I even wore T-shirts that were a part of my regular everyday wardrobe with sayings reflecting my faith. I read my Bible in the locker room, listened to gospel music, and prayed before practice and games. Surprisingly, my teammates were very receptive of my faith and would approach me from time to time to ask me some questions about it and the Bible. Many of them were searching for something spiritual in life and seemed genuinely interested in what I had to share. If anyone asked a question about the hope that I had within me, I gave an answer based on what the Scripture said.

B-Love

My teammates said they respected me because they saw that I was at least trying to be for real about what I professed to believe. They knew I was not without sin in my life, and they knew I never tried to force the Bible down anyone's throats. Sometimes they made fun of me and called me names like Jesse Jackson, Reverend Ike, and Al Sharpton. Yet they were also protective of me—like the team little brother—when it came to opponents trying to get a little too physical on the basketball court. They would always take up for me and make sure I was okay.

They nick named me B-Love, borrowed from the character Martin Lawrence played in the movie *House Party*. They gave me that moniker because I was always trying to show the love of Christ to everyone. My coach, on the other hand, was not so receptive towards my zeal for the Lord. One day while he was drawing up plays on the chalk board in the locker room, I was reading my Bible before practice. One of my teammates came in and asked me what I was reading. I gave him the biblical perspective, when my coach, who was listening, jumped in and swore, "That's bull s#@! I don't agree with that." I was shocked. I had never heard any one in my life refer to the things of God in that manner, and to be as disrespectful as that coach was. Interestingly, after that I was used sparingly if at all. I began wondering if the profession of my faith had anything to do with it, but I could not imagine being persecuted for sharing something so wonderful and important. It was not that I was trying to convert my teammates or the coaches, but that I was just very bold and outward (I hope in a nonjudgmental and noncritical way) about the God who had done so much for me. My personal philosophy had always been that if everyone else has the right to live as they please, and not apologize to anyone for doing so, then I have the right to live for God and not apologize for doing so.

I worked very hard at every practice and did well, but when game time came around I did not see much action. I began just going through the motions in practice because I saw no use in working hard every day and doing better than guys who were playing in front of me and yet still not getting the opportunity to play. My dad often came to my practices, and he noticed my lack of enthusiasm. He encouraged me to continue working hard if I wanted to have any chance of getting into the games. Two months went by, and I noticed I had not seen my dad at any of my practices. He would attend the games, but I was still not playing very much. We played against former NBA player Terry Dehere and the Seton Hall Pirates on ESPN, with Dick Vitale as the commentator. I was itching to get in. I had not gotten in the game by half time and my dad was so frustrated he came down behind the bench to talk to the coach about why I had not been put in the game yet. He asked if I was injured. My dad did not understand why I was not getting in the game because he had been secretly coming to my practices the last two months and sitting out of sight, all the way up at the top of the field house. He wanted to see for himself what I was doing in practices and why I was not being allowed to contribute to the team during games.

He told the coach at half time that he had been following me in practice for two months and watching me dunk on our 6'11" center, Spencer Dunkley, who eventually got drafted to the NBA. He could not understand what the problem was. Now maybe that was not the right time to hold a meeting with the coach, but I guess it worked. I got in the second half of the game. I only scored one point, which was a foul shot, and I did not play very long at all. By this time the coach had conditioned me to expect to hear a buzzer and be substituted if I shot the ball. I felt like a Pavlovian salivating dog experiment; each time I heard the substitution buzzer, I just turned and headed for the bench—whether or not he was even bringing me out of the game. At any rate, I began wondering if professing my faith had something to do with my not being given much of a chance to play. Would someone keep me from playing a game I loved so much because of what I believed?

Going Downhill

Basketball was not going well, and generally things began going further downhill. Trying to find encouragement in the situation, I went to do my devotions one day, but my Bible was missing from my desk. I used to leave it on the left edge of the desk in my room, above a trash can I emptied regularly. It occurred to me that maybe the Bible fell in the trash can and I threw it out by mistake. I did not replace it and my daily devotions, which were consistent up until then, had stopped all together. Instead of replacing my Bible right away and turning to the Word to fill the void, I turned to other sources. Now that basketball was not able to bring fulfillment, I started attending the college campus parties to feel a sense of acceptance and significance. I do thank God that I did not start drinking or taking drugs, or anything like that, but my teammates were there and everybody knew who we were. It did not help that we got into all the parties for free, no matter who was hosting them. I must admit they were fun at first, but after a while the parties lost the excitement. The same people were at all of them, dancing to the same songs, and always getting drunk. I found myself slowly but surely becoming a wall flower. The last party I went to sent me straight to the wall the moment I got in. I looked around and thought that this was not for me. I lost the desire and left after being there for about ten or fifteen minutes.

The surprising thing was that I did not even go to parties in high school. I went to one senior fellowship at the end of the year, but that was about it. I knew in my heart the party scene was not me. Still trying to fill the void, I ran into my ex-girlfriend in the library, and I turned back to the relationship with her for comfort. I wanted to have some balance in my life by having something other than basketball to look forward to. It was like old times. We grew very close again and spent a lot of time together. I know now that I was using this relationship to try to fill the empty space left by basketball, and it worked temporarily. But God wanted me to fill the void with him and his presence, not relationships or anything else.

I began spending a lot of time at her dorm, and we watched movies that made us laugh and we really enjoyed one another's company—just like we did when we were in high school. Eventually, we became intimate sexually again and sometimes I spent the night with her in her room. I know that I should not have put myself in that situation, but I did. And afterwards, I felt the same way as before, always feeling joyless, guilty, and rotten. My Christian peace and zeal was gone each time it happened.

I should have been tired of the emotional roller coaster. I brought all of this on myself because I was making bad decisions, and once again I had betrayed the God who had blessed me tremendously. That relationship did not last as expected, and we broke up shortly thereafter, this time for good. After going solo for a while I got into another relationship with another young lady and vowed to not repeat the same sinful behavior. The same sinful pattern followed, however. By this time, the first half of the basketball season was over and the relationship went on into the second semester. Besides living a sexually impure life, my grades had slipped to the point where I almost flunked out of school. My coach, who rarely had anything to say to me, teased me at practice by saying, "I can see the headlines now. Kevin Benton, Philadelphia Public League Player of the Year, flunks out of school." I was able to put two and two together and figured God was trying to get my attention by allowing the trouble in my life. I certainly did not want my family to ever have to read that headline.

One of the hardest decisions I ever had to make was to break off the relationship with this new girlfriend. At first, she did not take it well, but she eventually understood my reasons. She said, "I know you're doing this because you are trying to be a good Christian." We still remained good friends, with no animosity or hard feelings, but the dynamics of our friendship changed dramatically. At this point I was not going to any more parties, or even dating for that matter. It was just going to be me and God, books, and basketball. I was still depressed and discouraged as I assessed my life at that time, and I wondered if it was even worth trying to live right when I was being stripped of the things I loved. I know now that God wanted to be first in my life and at that time, he came in third or fourth. Basketball was an idol. It was who I was. I learned later that God used my coach to allow basketball to be infringed upon. He did this because he loved me to the point that he did not want my self esteem and self worth to be wrapped up in anything that was susceptible to change. Why? Because God knew I would have been destroyed by those very things. He wanted me to be wrapped up in him and him alone.

Entertaining Angels

I went for a walk one night around the perimeter of the campus and wrestled with suicidal thoughts. I was angry at God, myself, and life in general for feeling a sense of failure. When I came to the end of the road I saw a Caucasian man in a suit with a small box in one hand and a small square green thing in the other. I could not make out what he was holding. As I continued moving in his direction, I noticed what he had in his hands was a box of little green Gideon Bibles. He handed one to me as I walked by him. I only took about three steps before saying to myself, "A Bible—I needed one of these. I'm going to go back and thank the man." When I turned around, he was gone.

I never saw him again. I personally believe this figure was an angel sent by God. The writer of Hebrews says, "Do not forget to entertain strangers, for by so doing some have unwittingly entertained angels" (13:2).

I put the Bible in my pocket and finished my walk, and from that night on I began doing my devotions regularly again. I even took some summer classes to add to the ones I took during winter break to help bring my grades up. Gratefully, I did not flunk out. Even though the outlook for basketball still did not look promising for me (especially since we had six seniors returning next season), God began restoring me back to that place in him.

I knew in my heart that I still should have been getting playing time. I was a part of Delaware's most highly touted freshman basketball class in the history of the school. That summer I sought the Lord by fasting and praying and asking for direction on whether I should transfer to Drexel in Philadelphia, go to another school, or go back to the University of Delaware. I felt God wanted me to go back to Delaware, so in obedience to that I did, even though I did not want to.

When I returned the following year for my sophomore campaign, things began getting even worse. After praying and discussing it with my family, I decided I should sit out and redshirt my sophomore season. Redshirting simply means that the NCAA allows student athletes five years of scholarship eligibility in order to play four years. To redshirt would have allowed for me to sit out a year while continuing to practice with the team, and then the next year, when the six seniors would have graduated, there would be no reason for me not to get some playing time. My coach agreed with this thinking and approved the plan. I trained hard every day and practiced with the team, and when the season came around I did not play in any of the games. I must admit it was very hard sitting on the bench in street clothes watching when I wanted to be out there playing. I just had to keep remembering that the decision to sit out would be good for my future in basketball. With no help from me, the team advanced to the NCAA tournament to play against former NBA player Nick Van Excel and the Cincinnati Bear Cats.

Panic Attacks

This particular year, instead of having a roommate, I lived in a single dorm because I wanted to better concentrate and focus on the Lord, school, and basketball training. I was back to reading my Bible consistently every chance I got. I began developing a hunger and thirst for the Word of God. My outward profession of faith did not change around my teammates at practices, in the classroom, around campus, or in the dorm. But in the dorm I began to run into some problems. There were only two African American students living on our floor—me and the other person living directly across the hall from me. The Caucasian students ran the other African American student out of the dorm because when our RA was not there, which was often, they would spit on his door and do things like rip his posters off his door and pour water under his door. I guess he got tired of it and moved out, and I did not blame him. Seeing this, I became very angry and determined they would not run me off the same way. But sure enough, they started working on me as soon as the other black student was gone. They would prank call me at 3:00 AM to wake me up, or knock on my door and run during the wee hours of the morning. The guy living next to me had two concert size speakers in his room and would blast his music so loud I could not hear myself think. Just about every day I had to go next door and ask him to turn his music down—which he would do for a brief period of time before turning it sky-high again.

I could not tell the RA because he was never around. I did not feel I could talk to my coach about this because the way he was treating me with basketball I felt he would not care. I even thought of taking matters into my own hands and punching a few of the guys out, but that idea was discarded because I was trying to be conscious of my testimony. Also, the headlines about me getting expelled from school crossed my mind and I did not want to embarrass my family. All of this added up and became psychological torment because I was going through this day in and day out. After my classes were over, I looked forward to going to basketball practice so I did not have to deal with the situation at the dorm. Yet fear always came over me when the practices were finished. I kept wondering, "What will I have to deal with today"? I became angry and bitter at those students on the floor who were treating me this way, and I was tempted on many occasions to act out, even though I knew this was wrong because of my professing outwardly to being a Christian. I tried very hard to maintain my testimony both on and off the court, even though I was not successful all the time.

I was not getting much sleep. When I did eventually fall asleep, I would wake up in the middle of the night in cold sweats with my heart beating really fast. This continued for a while and my body began feeling run-down and sickly. I went to the doctor down at the basketball field house for a checkup. As I was sitting in the waiting room, all of a sudden my heart started palpitating really quickly and it felt like it was about to come out of my chest. I saw yellow and black spots before my eyes, and I yelled for the doctor as I felt like I was about to black out. I got dizzy, felt hot flashes, had shortness of breath, and had a tingling sensation in my hands, arms, legs, and feet. I felt like I was losing control of my body and mind. The doctors hurried to my side and took me in the back room for a physical. In the end they told me I was fine and that what I had was a panic attack. These are short periodic spurts of panic that occur suddenly, reach a peak within ten minutes, and then gradually pass. To me, thinking I was having a heart attack and dying, those ten minutes or so felt like an eternity.

The doctors told me to relax and sent me on my way back to the dorm, where I did not want to go in the first place. As I was walking home from the field house and going over the bridge leading to the part of campus where all the dorms were, a truck went flying by and the bridge started shaking. I got very scared; my legs got weak, and my heart starting beating fast again. Again I felt like I was going to black out, and then I collapsed on the bridge. Someone called an ambulance and they rushed me to the hospital. I had had another panic attack, but this one was a little worse than the first one. I had developed what they called a panic disorder, which is having repeated and sudden panic attacks without apparent reasons.

My family was notified and they rushed to the hospital. When my dad walked into my hospital room, he came over to the bed were I was lying, kissed me on the cheek, and said, "Just don't give up." That was the first time he had kissed me since I was young. I stayed at the hospital for a few days, left school, and went back home to Philadelphia. I just lay on the coach for days at a time and wondered what was going on in my life and why God was allowing this to happen to me. I had another anxiety attack on the porch of my house while my mom and dad were at work. My next door neighbor called the ambulance and this time they rushed me to the intensive care unit of the University of Pennsylvania hospital. My family was more concerned this time than the first time I was admitted in Delaware. My coach called to ask me if I thought I would be able to make it back for the next season. Knowing the seriousness of my condition and lacking faith in me, he went out that summer and began recruiting for my position for the following year. I did not hold that against him because I was not playing much anyway, and he was just doing his job. To be honest, even I did not have confidence I was going to make it back next season. While in the ICU, a team of doctors tried to determine my diagnosis and kept telling me, "We're going to get you back out on that court, so don't worry."

After running an EKG they determined I had a rare heart disease found in African American males. It is called hypertrophic-cardiomyopathy, and it is the same heart disease that basketball player Willie "Scoops" Cager (played by actor Damaine Radcliff) had in the movie *Glory Road.* But my condition was a lot worse. My hypertrophic-cardiomyopathy caused my heart to enlarge and send blood flowing in the wrong direction, sometimes through the valves, causing fast palpitations, dizziness, and weakness in the limbs. And, of course, all the panic attack symptoms. I had a faint pulse and my blood pressure was very low. In about a month I had dropped from 190 pounds with two percent body fat down to 140 pounds, where you could see my rib cage and I could barely walk. The doctors told my family they had done what could be done and that they could do nothing more. My mother was crying by my bedside and she said, "Good, now let go and let God." My dad came over to kiss me on the cheek again before they left for the day. He told me again, "Just don't give up." I did not know at the time that the doctors had given me one day to live due to my serious condition. That night, I lay on my hospital bed hooked up to a machine that monitored my heart. I wrestled with God and questioned why his Word said "The steps of a good man are ordered by the Lord, and He delights in his way" (Psalm 37:23).

God Was Not Finished with Me Yet

How could a loving God allow, let alone order, something like this in my life when I was at least trying to take a stand for him, trying to do right, and trying to do his will? I was not perfect, and I never used my imperfection as an excuse, but I was trying to be a good witness. I could not come to grips with the fact that this was the way that my life was going to end. I began reading the Bible throughout the day and listening to Christian television stations. Every message I turned on was about how God was going to heal me and raise me up off of my bed of affliction because he was not finished with me yet. I just knew these preachers were talking specifically to me and my situation. And needing a word of encouragement, especially at that time, I took those words to heart. When I woke up on the second day in the hospital, I was surprised that I had lived through the night. I praised and thanked God for another day that was not promised, and I whispered to myself, "The dream is still alive. I've still got time left on the clock." So I decided then to praise and thank God every day that he wakes me up in the morning. That same day, while I was lying awake in the bed, an old cleaning lady mopped her way into my room. She put her mop down next to my bed, grabbed me by the hands, and began praying for me in the name of Jesus Christ. I don't remember everything she said, but I do remember her praying with an African accent. "God, in the name of Jesus, heal him because the devil is trying to take his life because he has a calling on his life. And God, use him for your praise, honor, and glory."

When she finished praying, a peace came over my entire body as if someone had poured cold water on me from my head that slowly trickled down to my feet. Tears flowed from my eyes because of her gesture of love. The old lady left the room, and I never saw her again. When the doctor came in to take my blood pressure, he was amazed at the results. He said, "I don't understand what just happened," as he kept looking at the pressure gauge to make sure it was working properly and that he was reading it correctly.

Even though he saw major improvement in my condition, he wanted me to stay in the hospital one more day. Another EKG showed the size of my heart had gone down, and my appetite started to come back. I knew for sure that God had miraculously healed my body and raised me up from my bed of affliction as the television preachers said he would do. I came into the intensive care unit in a wheelchair, and now two days later I was walking out after being released to go home due to my improved condition. My appetite had returned and I began gaining my weight back slowly but surely.

It seems that when I read Psalm 37:23, "The steps of a good man are ordered by the Lord, and He delights in his way," I had failed to read the next verse, "Though he fall, he shall not be utterly cast down: For the Lord upholds him with His hand." The Word of God connected with my personal traumatic experience, letting me know that a loving God allowed me to go through what I went through. He loved me and did not leave me hanging. At this point I stopped questioning why God allowed me to go through what I went through and began questioning myself as to why he allowed me to survive it. I knew if I could answer this second question I could figure out what my destiny in Christ was. There simply had to be a purpose.

Road to Recovery

My battle with depression and panic attacks was not completely over when I got home from the hospital. I stayed in the house all day because I was still afraid to be by myself for fear I would collapse or that something bad would happen to me when no one was around to help. My panic disorder was now combined with agoraphobia, the fear of being in places or situations where escape might be difficult. So I just lounged around on the couch day in and day out for about a month, becoming dependent on my anti-anxiety medications. The medicine for me became like a security blanket.

One morning my mother came downstairs and told me God had revealed to her that I was healed. My dad also shared his concern for my lack of movement when he challenged me to get up and get back into the swing of things. Time was flying because life was slowly passing me by.

The next morning my mother came down stairs again but this time she grabbed my basketball and then grabbed me by the hand as she pulled me off the couch and said, "Come on, get up. We are going over to the playground." I was scared and really did not want to go in fear that I would collapse and die. My mother held my hand and guided me comparable to when I was a little helpless child. Even though I was a grown man, like a little helpless child, I allowed myself to be slowly led by her all the way to the playground. When we finally arrived she told me to start shooting around while she grabbed the rebounds. The more I began to shoot around and nothing happened to me, the more confident I became. The interesting thing about this particular scenario was that I had the comfort of knowing that someone was there with me in the event that something happened. The real test for me was going to be attempting to do this again but all by myself.

The following morning, while I was at home alone, I decided to pick up my ball and take a slow and gingerly long walk to Johnson's playground. I went back to the place where I started playing basketball as a youngster. I guess it was kind of like Superman returning to Krypton to get his powers back. I was scared to death as thoughts of collapsing tormented my mind. But I decided God had my life in his hands, so I kept on walking. Whatever he allows, he allows. And besides, if God wanted me dead, he had had plenty of opportunities to allow that to happen while I was hospitalized. Once I made it to the basketball courts, I began shooting around. The longer I played with nothing bad happening, the more confidence I gained. After this, I began visiting the courts every day by myself for practice. I had lost a lot of muscle mass and weight, but I knew I was on the road to recovery.

The Delaware coaches wanted to have a meeting with me and my family at the field house to determine my future as a University of Delaware student athlete. My coach, who had a master's degree in psychology, opened the meeting by suggesting I go to a psychiatrist for further help and evaluation. All of a sudden my dad threw his Bible on the middle of the table in front of this meeting of about ten people and said, "We believe the Bible is the blueprint for life, and we are not sending Kevin to a secular psychiatrist. If we do send him anywhere, we are sending him to a Christian counselor." All of their faces displayed a look of shock, and their mouths sat wide open. I am sure some of the coaching staff were thinking, "Oh no, not his family, too." My coach turned bright red as he grabbed his face in disgust. Our team wellness professor, Dr. Janice Jordan, turned to me and said, "Well, Kevin, what do you have to say?" I responded, with basketball in hand, "This is a path that God has allowed in my life to make me stronger." Then I paused and said, "I'll be back." Dr. Jordan said, "That concludes our meeting. Thank you all for coming," after which everyone moved out in silence.

Peace, Be Still

My family and I sought out Pastors Dr. Clarence and Dr. Ja'Ola Walker, who had a family therapy and counseling practice on City Line Avenue in Philadelphia, directly across the street from St. Josephs University. I attended sessions with Dr. Clarence Walker once a week and continued taking an anti-anxiety medicine. I slowly but surely began improving. The Scripture Dr. Walker based my therapy and meditation on was found in the gospel of Mark, when Jesus calmed the storm on the sea: "Then he arose and rebuked the wind, and said to the sea, 'Peace, be still!' And the wind ceased and there was a great calm" (4:39).

Pastor Walker had me meditate on this story along with this particular verse so that Jesus might speak to the storm in my mind and bring a great calm. He also gave me muscle tension relaxation training exercises and instructed me to take hot baths to relieve anxiety. The rationale for this was that physical relaxation would lead to a state of psychological relaxation. Also, he instructed me to take the medicine only if I needed it. I followed his orders and God continued healing and restoring me spiritually, mentally, emotionally, and physically during that summer. In my particular case, the various approaches he used to treat me proved that a multiplicity of psychological approaches yields better results.

The Ultimate Heart Fixer

The Sonny Hill college summer basketball league at Temple University was considered one of the top three summer leagues in the country. I was worried about playing in the league due to my health condition. As the time for the league was approaching, I was not as concerned about having panic attacks as I was about what kind of physical shape I could get in before it started. On top of this, the competition was very tough. The players from all of the area big five schools (Temple, LaSalle, Drexel, Penn, and Villanova) played in this league, not to mention pro prospects like my high school rival and good friend Aaron McKie, who played for Temple University. Eddie Jones of Temple played in the league also, who had a nice career in the NBA as well. Even though I did not get a chance to train and prepare as I would have liked to, I decided to play anyway and have the chance to reunite with my brother David and my cousin Brian Benton.

To my surprise every week I saw God strengthening my body as I began getting faster and jumping higher and eventually, as the summer progressed, pretty much dismantling the league. The game that confirmed to me that God helped me overcome my condition and restored my health was when we played against Eddie Jones's team. We both played very well and it made for an entertaining game for those who watched. At the conclusion of the game, my brother and I walked towards the locker rooms. We heard an announcement that came from the scores table. The announcer said, "Tonight's leading scorers, Eddie Jones, 33 points, and Kevin Benton, 33 points." My brother reiterated to me what the announcer had just said, "Kev, you and Eddie both had 33." I was very surprised and encouraged and realized that I did something special, especially considering what I had recently experienced with my health. Playing the way I did that evening made me realize for sure that I could play in the NBA. I was the third leading scorer in the league that year with 20.3 average points per game.

I happened to look up into the stands during another one of the games to see my assistant coach from the University of Delaware. He had heard about all the publicity I was getting in the league and he came to see for himself, especially since the last time he saw me I was in very poor health. I played extremely well that game and scored twenty-one points against Aaron McKie's team. After the game was over I watched my coach storm out of the balcony of Temple's McGonagall Hall gym. It was as if he had some news to report to somebody. I knew the first person he probably would call was the head coach to give him the update.

The summer was over and it was time to head back to school. I was still a sophomore by basketball eligibility standards, due to the fact that I sat out the previous year. My healing was a blessing because if I was still sick I would have lost a year of scholarship eligibility to sit out another year while trying to recover. Basketball training began the week we arrived on campus as we took our pre-season physical fitness test. When I took the test I had improved and gotten stronger and faster in every area. My bench press increased, my vertical jump increased, my speed increased, and I was healthy and in great shape—all to the praise, honor, glory, and credit of Jesus Christ. The Lord not only miraculously healed me but strengthened me as well.

Once the season started, everyone agreed I should be in the starting lineup this year due to the improvement I made and the six seniors who had graduated and moved on. Everyone, that is, except the head coach. Surprisingly, he left off right where he did the year prior to me redshirting and sitting out. It was like he refused to see me get any credit. I was still me, and maybe that was the problem. I was still the Christian who was unashamed of the gospel. I still prayed before stepping on the court, read the Word in the locker room, and wore my Christian message T-shirts.

The University of Delaware had just built the John Carpenter Center, the new basketball facility, and we had our first preseason inter-squad game of the blue team versus the gold team. Prior to the game the coach called me into his personal locker room where he was getting dressed to ask me some questions. He asked me how I felt physically, and I told him I felt great. He grabbed my bicep and squeezed as if he had to touch my more defined arm for himself, almost as if to see how real it was. He asked me what I did to continue my treatment throughout the summer for my panic attack condition, and I told him about my experience with the Christian therapist and family counselor, Dr. Clarence Walker. He could think what he wanted, but my presence alone was confirmation that God is who he says he is, the ultimate heart fixer and mind regulator. I did not care if the coach accepted my miracle testimony or not, because I was irrefutable evidence (along with some left over anti-anxiety pills that I still had and decided to keep as a memento for the rest of my life) of the power of God. God used me as a trophy as I was a living witness to the coach. As I walked out of his locker room I said to myself, "All I can do is tell him the truth. I'm not going to be ashamed of what God did for me."

Same Old Same Old

Once the inter-squad game started, the ball was passed to me. I went in for a vicious two-handed dunk, scoring the first unofficial basket in the new Carpenter Center facility. When the papers interviewed my coach after the game, he changed the story and gave credit to another player for scoring the first basket. My teammates were talking about it in the locker room the next day, and they admitted that that was wrong of the coach, but I just tried to be quiet and keep my focus. Once the season started it was the same old same old routine of not getting into games, but I knew when conference games came around we had to win, and I was prepared to play. The coach did not have all the seniors this year so he couldn't keep me out of the game for too long. I still continued working very hard every day in practice, especially as we began moving into the tougher scheduled games. With the conference games being the most important, my role got upgraded, just as I anticipated.

I was put in when I was needed to help bring us back from behind, and then it was back to the bench.

We were playing a conference game against a division rival and they were winning by ten points late in the game. Even then the coach was hesitant about putting me in, but finally he relented. Coming down court shooting the ball with nothing to lose, I scored eleven points in about a three minute time span, and by the time I scored my eleventh point, a foul shot, we were up by one point. Predictably, the buzzer sounded and back to the bench I went. We won the game, but when they interviewed my coach, again he did not even mention my name, choosing once more to give the credit to another teammate. The teammate the coach gave credit to even admitted to me in the locker room—in front of the entire team—that he did not win the game but that I did. I figured the coach wanted to continue persecuting me because of my faith, and because he did not want me to play professionally.

My dream was always to play in the NBA. Whenever I had short conversations with my coach about basketball, he would constantly tell me I was not good enough to play professional ball, that I was not strong enough, and that I should focus on getting my education so I could find a good job. After a stellar summer league season in the prestigious and highly touted Sonny Hill College League, I refused to believe him. I know now that when God gives you a dream or a vision, the best thing to do is to keep it to yourself until it is his time to reveal it. One of the most notable examples in the Bible of someone exposing their dreams prematurely was Joseph. As a result, he experienced jealousy from his brothers, who tried to kill him and then threw him into a pit. I did not know why I was being thrown into a symbolic pit by my coach; it was a hard one to figure out.

One of our inner-state rivalries was the Delaware State University Hornets. While we were on the bus heading down to the game, one of my teammates asked me a theological question about salvation in connection with going to heaven or hell. My response was simple and plain: "According to what the Bible says, if you admit you are a sinner and receive Jesus Christ as your personal Savior, you will spend eternity in heaven with him when you die. And if you don't receive Christ as your personal Savior, you will go to hell for eternity when you die." Some of my teammates began chiming in and asking questions to refute what I said, but I stuck to my guns and even used Scripture to support my claim. They did not try to argue the topic with me, but instead we respectfully went back and forth with the discussion. Interestingly, despite a somewhat tense atmosphere on the bus, the coach remained quiet and did not try saying anything like he did in the locker room two years before. In any case, we arrived at the gym and got ready to play the game.

The game was a good one. DSU jumped out to an early lead, and I began preparing myself mentally to get in the game and save the day. It is a shame that I had to anticipate playing under these circumstances, but this was the only reason I was put in the game, and I picked up on the pattern after a while. Sure enough, my coach looked down the bench and was hesitant to put me in, but finally he gave in to the situation. As soon as the buzzer sounded, I walked from the score table onto the floor, and then I heard my coach say, "No, no, no, Kevin. Come on back out." I went back to the bench wondering what that was all about. I never got back in, and we lost the game.

Hardening Hearts

My dad told me he had been praying and fasting back home and that God led him to the story of Moses and Pharaoh in the Scriptures, which he likened to my situation. Little did he know that God had led me to that same passage that week. I knew for sure I was being persecuted for the stand I was taking for Jesus Christ. The testimony of my comeback defied my coach's logic and made him even more inflexible. After the DSU game my dad, realizing what was going on spiritually, had a few choice words to say to the coach. He was never afraid to speak up about the way he felt, but I must admit that sometimes I wondered if he was not helping the situation. Coaches have been known to take things out on a player because of the type of relationship they have or don't have with parents or family members. However, now God was revealing to both of us that my coach's heart was hardened and that no matter what we did or said, it really did not matter. God confirmed this to us during our separate fasting and prayer times that week. In Exodus 4:21, we read, "And the Lord said to Moses, 'When you go back to Egypt, see that you do all those wonders before Pharaoh which I have put in your hand. But I will harden his heart, so that he will not let the people go.'"

God does not make soft hearts hard but instead takes hearts that are already hard and makes them harder because of their rebellion. In the end, God uses hard-hearted people to accomplish his will. He still blesses and promotes his people by way of some painful situations. It did not matter what I did, the coach would have still treated me the same way—because this was God's doing. I caught the bus back to campus with the team and my dad drove so he could meet me back at my dormitory. When we met up at the dorm we talked about the situation and he began encouraging me to persevere. He told me "God is either going to move the coach, move you, or give you the strength to go through this. But he's going to do something, especially when the situation starts to go from bad to worse."

Oh Yeah, and One More Thing

I had had a very long day and was tired, weary, and worn out from continuously having to fight spiritually and mentally. I turned to my dad and said, "One day, I'm going to write a book about this stuff." At the time I was kidding around, but I made that statement based on reflecting back in disbelief about my entire experience at the University of Delaware from the time I arrived on campus until that very day. After my dad left to go back to Philadelphia, I began preparing for bed. As soon as I fell asleep that night I had an encounter with God in a vision that terrified me. In Job 4:12-16, the Bible says, "Now a word was secretly brought to me, And my ears received a whisper of it. In disquieting thoughts from the visions of night, When deep sleep falls on men, Fear came upon me, and trembling, Which made all my bones shake. Then a spirit passed before my face; The hair on my body stood up. It stood still, But I could not discern its appearance. A form was before my eyes; There was silence; Then I heard a voice."

The vision started out in my dorm room, and the exact way that my room was set up in real life was the way it appeared in the vision. In the vision, while lying in bed asleep, I was awakened by fear and shortness of breath as my stomach began to tighten. I felt myself descending downward. The feeling was comparable to being on an elevator going from the top floor of a tall building all the way down to the bottom floor, only faster. Just as an elevator would, my bed seemed to land softly on the ground as it came to a stop. Once I stopped descending, I was terrified by a horrifying presence. The presence was so frightening and horrifying that I stayed under the covers as if to be able to hide. The presence surrounding me felt like death and like I was about to die but could not. I was so terrified that I started crying and was literally shaking with fear. I peeked out from under the covers and I saw large orange fiery flames surrounding my bed in a perfect full circle as my bed was positioned in the middle of a valley. I could only vaguely see beyond the flames, because the flames were very large and past my direct line of vision. Trying to see what was beyond the flames, I just saw the fumes from the fire that made whatever was behind the flames very blurry. The color of the background was pitch black with the only light being provided by the flames that surrounded my bed. I quickly pulled the covers back over my head again and continued crying, shaking, and shivering with fear. Besides the feeling of horror, terror, and indescribable fear, seeing the large orange flames and the fumes that permeated from them, I felt extreme heat. I realized that God had taken my bed out of my dorm room and placed it in hell—in my vision, I was in hell. The interesting thing in all of this was that even though I was experiencing these characteristics of hell, I felt in my heart that these were not the only ones, even though I did not see anything else. A great part of the sense of fear that I was experiencing was the anticipation of the unexpected and the unknown. I knew something else was out there—I just didn't know what. It brought immense fear over me to know that I could be harmed. On the other hand, I also felt protected. It seemed like nothing could come past the perfect full circle of fire that surrounded my bed. I also felt in my heart that in a sense, I was not experiencing these aspects of hell to the highest degree. Despite what I was experiencing, I knew for some odd reason that God's presence was there with me as I was lying in bed frightened under those covers. It was almost as if God wanted me to know that he was there with me but at the same time he pulled back his presence to an extent. He wanted to allow me to experience some of what it felt like to be tormented in hell so I would know that it was really real.

I know it was not God's presence that caused me to be so horrified "for God has not given us a spirit of fear but of power and of love and of a sound mind" (2 Tim. 1:7). The only fear that God's presence invokes is the type of fear which is reverence or holy fear. To add to this, "In Your presence is the fullness of joy" (Ps. 16:11). In fact, when we come into God's presence, the first thing that it makes us want to do is fall down and worship him. What I was experiencing was far from having power because I felt powerless and hopeless in my surroundings. And it was far from feeling love and having a sound mind because I was so terrified. I definitely did not feel the fullness of joy but rather the fullness of fear and horror and this certainly did not make me want to worship but weep.

Some people may have a problem with God's presence being in hell with me because hell is separation from God, and his presence is not there. However, God being God, he promises his children, "I will never leave you nor forsake you" (Heb. 13:5). Even though I was in hell, I still knew for certain that I was a child of God and that the omnipresent God was still with me as I laid in my bed frightened almost to death. I knew right then and there that there was nowhere I could go as a believer that the presence of God would not be with me. Psalm 139:8-10 assured me of this. "If I ascend into heaven, You are there; If I make my bed in hell, behold, You are there, If I take the wings of the morning, And dwell in the uttermost parts of the sea, Even there Your hand shall lead me, And your right hand shall hold me." In the gospel of Matthew I was given further assurance, "and lo, I am with you always, even to the end of the age" (10:28).

In my vision, a voice began speaking that sounded like rushing water, yet it was quiet and calm. The voice sounded like thousands of people speaking at the same time, synchronized and on cue, like a choir without missing a note. The voice said, "Whatever you do, don't ever give up because that's what the Devil wants you to do." I knew without question that this was the voice of God. I had been going through so much persecution with my coach, and with the way I was treated at the Delaware State game being the last straw, I was contemplating leaving school and going back home and taking a year off to rest from being so spiritually weary. The other reason I knew that this was the voice of God is because the Devil would never tell me not to give up. Giving up is what the Enemy wants us to do. Jesus even told us in his Word, that every kingdom divided against itself is brought to desolation, and every city or house divided against itself will not stand (Matt. 12:25). So with full assurance of who it was, I responded while still under the covers and said, "I'm not going to give up. I'm just resting, that's all." And then the voice said, "Oh yeah, and one more thing…"

I was so anxious to hear what the one more thing was that God wanted to tell me that I snapped out of the vision and woke up. I knew in my heart that what he was about to tell me was significant, and in line with my dream and destiny. But he didn't reveal it to me. The vision was gone. For many years after that, I thought that God was going to tell me I would make it to the NBA, because that was my dream and that was what I wanted to hear him say. But it was not his dream and his purpose for me. When the NBA did not pan out for me, I felt a sense of incompleteness and wanted to know what that "one more thing" was that God wanted me to know and wanted me to do. So my search in life continued on.

When I woke up after my vision, my heart was beating very fast, I was breathing very hard, and I was sweating profusely. As I lay there in bed trying to make sense of what just happened, my entire body was numb. I raised my head up and looked down my body and began poking my chest and stomach until a sense of feeling came back. I looked over at my dorm radiator to see if I had slept with the heat up high as I did most nights. I saw that it was in the off position. This vision happened during the 1992-1993 academic year, and I have spent the rest of my life since then trying to figure out what was the one more thing that God wanted me to know or do. I believe that I certainly know now.

Now Is the Time

Years later, married and living in Philadelphia, I remember coming home from church one day a little discouraged. While reflecting, I was not sure about the direction I should be going in my life. As I walked into the house I whispered to God that I really needed to hear an encouraging word from him. Believing I could always hear a good word from the Lord on TBN, a worldwide Christian Broadcasting Network, I turned on the television. The channel was already set because my wife Nikki watched it every morning before going to work. The pastor on the screen spoke these words as it came on, "You have to prepare for the blessing, now is the time to start your ministry, now is the time to go back to school, now is the time to write the book, now is the time, now is the time, now is the time." I heard the message so plainly, as if the pastor was talking directly to me. He seemed to be looking straight at me as he looked into the camera and said those words. I knew God was using this pastor to speak to me. For years I told my wife that God was leading me to start a ministry, finish up a few classes I had left in order to complete my bachelor's degree, and write a book. It seemed that now was the time for procrastination to end.

The following Sunday my wife and I went to visit the largest megachurch in Philadelphia. The pastor began speaking about how in the latter days things were going to get worse before they got better. The entire sermon was awesome, but the point that stuck out to me the most was when he said, "Despite things getting worse in the latter days before they get better, now is the time to get into your gift so that you can do your part to make a difference for Jesus Christ." I knew that I had a gift to write and tell an interesting story. I figured I had an interesting life. After the service was over, my wife and I were walking back to our car. I told her that God confirmed that he wanted me to start a ministry, go back to school, and start writing my book. My wife, hearing me entertain these thoughts for years and finally deciding to act, responded with pleasure and support.

Having heard the revelation and confirmation, along with getting the other two tasks initiated, I began writing my book right away. When I first started writing, the direction I went was to explore why God allows suffering and pain in the lives of believers. As days went by, and after having finished my introduction and first chapter, God changed my direction and showed me that he wanted me to write about hell as the ultimate place of suffering and pain. He wanted me to write about my real experience there because people don't believe hell is real and are dying every day and going there. Even the church seems not fully persuaded of the reality of hell, and it does not have the broken heart for souls that it used to have.

I understood that because of my zeal and reckless boldness in college, God did not give me the total interpretation of my assignment in the vision. I probably would have gone to basketball practice the next day and told everyone that God took me to hell, that it really is a real place, and that they should get saved today in order to avoid going there. My coaches and teammates would have really thought I was fanatical and delusional, if they didn't think so already. I was not spiritually mature enough at that time to handle a revelation such as this, nor was I yet in a position to write a book of such magnitude.

Even with the visitation and revelation that God gave me, however, I was afraid to tell people for many years. I was afraid people would make fun of me and not believe I was telling the truth. Besides sharing this with my wife, who always believed in me and supported me, I have only shared this testimony once privately. It happened when my long time friend, Gerald Jordan, former Los Angeles Lakers and Harlem Globetrotter, told me of a vision God gave him about a job opportunity he was waiting on and asked me if I believed in visions. I responded that I did, and afterwards I proceeded to tell him about my visitation to hell. We encouraged one another and recognized that neither one of us was delusional.

I did not even share my testimony with my immediate family members. In fact, the first time I ever shared my testimony publically was at my little cousin Joseph "Boonie" Moore's funeral. Now a minister, I was responsible for doing the altar call portion of the service, and with the seriousness of the situation and people's eternity at stake, I seized the opportunity. With my immediate and non-immediate family in attendance, I shared my experience of visiting hell. I did not care if anyone believed me or not, but God gave me the fearless boldness to give my testimony anyway. Afterwards, I asked everyone in attendance to repeat the sinner's prayer silently in their hearts. I then prompted them to make a public profession of their decision. Thirteen people raised their hands to acknowledge receiving Christ. They came to the front of the church because they wanted to openly admit that they accepted Christ as their personal Savior. Some of the people who came to the front of the church included some of my own family members. I strongly believed that many other people in attendance received Christ but did not raise their hands. I told everyone that the most important thing was that they prayed the prayer with sincerity from their hearts. I also told them that God was the ultimate judge and that he knows our hearts. God confirmed to me that day that he had taken me to another level and that by writing this book I was on the right track and doing his will.

Two weeks after my cousin's funeral I was laying in bed one day reflecting on his life and all the fun times we had together hanging out and playing basketball. Having shared my vision at his funeral, I began to meditate on the vision. While contemplating, God began to give me the revelation as to the full meaning of the vision. I received an epiphany as I heard God's voice about what else he wanted to tell me before I suddenly woke up. God revealed that the fire represented his protection, and that despite what I was going through with my coach in college at that time, his presence would protect me. Further, as I passed through the fire of trials, troubles, and tribulations, and even hell, he would be with me. This is confirmed by the prophet Isaiah, who wrote, "When you pass through the waters, I will be with you; and through the rivers, they shall not overflow you. When you walk through the fire, you shall not be burned, nor shall the flame scorch you" (43:2).

Fire in the Bible can mean different things. It can mean affliction, as was just mentioned (Isa. 43:2). And it can mean protection, as was also just mentioned (Zech. 2:5). But fire can also represent persecution (Luke 12:49-53), purification (Isa. 6:5-7), and preservation from hell (Ps. 97:10). I could apply all of these symbolic representations of fire to the trials I went through in college. While there, these were the only revelations God brought to mind. But he has put the finishing touches on the vision I had in college by showing me that fire can represent so many more things, including God's vengeance (Heb. 12:29), God's wrath (Rom. 1:18), God's Word (Jer. 5:14), God's judgment (Rev. 18:8), God himself (Deut. 4:24), and God sentencing the wicked to hell (Jude 7).

The God whose fire would protect me from affliction and persecution would purify me as his child. That fire would be the same fire that would one day pour out his wrath, judgment, and vengeance on the wicked and the unrighteous, as one day they will be turned into hell (Ps.

9:17). While I was in hell, God's fiery protection shielded me from being harmed by hell's full effects. This was symbolic of being preserved from hell's fire, due to the free gift of salvation I had already received. Therefore, the birth of this book was an assignment given to me by God to witness to a dark and dying world heading straight to hell. I am also charged with challenging Christians to fulfill the "Great Commission" with a sense of urgency. Those who do not know Jesus Christ need to be told that they can repent and that their sins can be forgiven, and that coming to Christ is the only way to escape the vengeance, wrath, and judgment of hell that is coming.

I mentioned earlier that while in hell, the last thing I heard the voice of God say to me was "Oh yeah, and one more thing…" Being so anxious to hear what he had to say, I suddenly woke up. Many years later, I now know the meaning of the "one more thing" God wanted to tell me. Put very plainly, God wanted me to tell everyone that hell is a real place with real consequences and that no one should ever want to go there.

The search was over and the final piece of the puzzle was in place. I also found out something else God wanted to tell me. He gave me a word of knowledge, which is a word about future events, during my visitation in hell. I now have a sense of peace, contentment, and fulfillment in life that no NBA contract could ever bring, because I have realized my destiny and lifelong purpose. I finally found the abundant life. I know that a lot of money and material gain cannot bring complete happiness and fulfillment in life. If riches brought happiness, why would so many wealthy people commit suicide? This mission God gave me was much bigger than the NBA because I was given the opportunity to fulfill one of the greatest privileges one could ever be given on earth: to save people's lives and souls by leading them to the saving grace and knowledge of our Lord and Savior Jesus Christ.

God has given me a mission that is deep and wide, in line with my new dream and real destiny. It is to influence a dark and dying world for Jesus Christ, and I am humbled and honored that God, for whatever reason, chose me for such a task. Just as Ananias told Saul on the Damascus road about his encounter with God, "Then he said, 'The God of our fathers has chosen you that you should know His will, and see the Just One, and hear the voice of His mouth. For you will be His witness to all men of what you have seen and heard'" (Acts 22:14-15). The same applied to me, but the only difference was that when this happened to Saul he was not yet a believer. When it happened to me, I was.

I was escorted to hell in a vision and even though God did not allow me to experience the full magnitude of all the torments down there, the sheer horror was enough for me to let the whole world know that hell is a real place. God has instructed me to share that same word of knowledge he gave to me. This word now becomes a prophetic word of wisdom and warning to the world—hell is a real place and you do not ever want to go there.

CHAPTER THREE

Still Got the Blessing: What God has for Me is for Me

To conclude my brief experience at the University of Delaware, as my family and I continued praying and fasting about my future, my dad saw a rare commercial highlighting Liberty University, the largest evangelical Christian school in the world. The chancellor of the school was the late great Dr. Jerry Falwell, in my opinion one of the greatest Christian men of God to ever walk the face of the earth. It was an honor to have known him personally. The Lord compelled my dad's spirit that that was where I should be. Liberty had an awesome basketball program that was on the rise, and had some of the most beautiful facilities in the country. They had a basketball dome seating ten thousand, which sat in the middle of a beautiful campus. The next time my dad came to visit me at Delaware, he told me about what God had revealed to him. "If you want to be a Christian basketball player, I have just the place for you."

I did not know that my dad had already contacted the coaches at Liberty and told them that we would be interested in coming down for a visit in the next few days. But first we had to inform my coach at Delaware. My dad went into my coach's office and told him that our family did not see a future for me at Delaware, and that I would be leaving my scholarship there to enroll at Liberty University. I was waiting outside the office when my dad went in to talk to him. When he came back out he looked like he had seen a ghost. He said "K, I have never heard a voice like that come out of anybody before in my life. When I told him that we did not see a future for you here and that you would be transferring to Liberty, he got up and turned around to face the wall. With his back towards me, he said in a demonic voice, 'Get out!'"

We went back to my dorm room to pack all my belongings and headed to Lynchburg, Virginia, as we listened to the Delaware versus Vermont game on the radio. The situation just about broke me, and I was so spiritually drained from the last two and a half years at Delaware. I had peace but some mixed emotions as we drove off the campus for the last time, relieved that that sad chapter of my life was over. I had been on such an emotional roller coaster from all of this that I slept the entire five hours until we got to Lynchburg.

God showed us that things were not going to change that semester at Delaware, and that staying there would have been time wasted. He also showed us that if I had stayed at Delaware for my final two years, things still would not have changed for me because of what was in my coach's heart. I felt like my back was against a wall and an immediate escape was necessary so that the rest of my future would not be infringed upon. God came through again in the clutch.

Arriving at Liberty

We arrived that night at Liberty University and they already had a dorm room set up for me. My dad and I met with the coaches the next day. We told them our story of persecution at Delaware and how I wanted to be at a Christian school to play basketball. The head coach was Jeff Myers, who kept saying, "I can't believe you're sitting right here." My dad and I asked him why he kept saying that. Coach Myers said, "We borrowed some film last week so that we could scout a team we will be playing this weekend, and on the film the team we scouted happened to be playing against the University of Delaware. That's where I saw you, and now you're sitting right here." What worked in my favor this initial meeting was that the film the Liberty staff watched, recorded one of my best games of that season at Delaware. It happened to be the game that I scored eleven points in about three minutes, single-handedly bringing us back to the win column. So they were able to see what I could do. Randy Dunton was the assistant coach at the time, and he had some conduct concerns since I was now at a Christian School. I understood and did not take it personally because I knew of the negative examples some Philadelphia basketball players set at universities across the country. I did not have a problem with that or the many rules and regulations upheld by the Christian standard of the school. In fact, it was what I wanted.

Coach Myers tried reaching out to my coach at the University of Delaware. He told me that the UD coach did not have a lot of nice things to say about me. In interviews, the UD coach even lied about why I left Delaware. He said that I transferred to follow in the footsteps of my dad, who was a minister. This was not true as he was not a minister at the time (he was a deacon in our local church).

My coach at Delaware had plenty of opportunities to use me yet he did not. I could never understand why they recruited me in the first place. Sometimes I felt like Delaware recruited me so that I would not go to Drexel University. Coaches will sometimes try turning an athlete into a practice player to make the other guys on the team a little better. That is certainly what happened to me at UD. Another reason I think that Delaware wanted me was because I was the ticket to getting Philadelphia ball players. The one thing my coach did not take into consideration was that I was "Player of the Year" in Philadelphia, and if I was not getting playing time, no Philadelphia ball players would want to go to UD.

It was not hard to understand why Coach Felton, the top assistant coach who recruited me, left. Looking back, I sometimes wish I had gone to Tulane where he was. When someone does not want to receive your God-given gifts, talents, and ability, the Lord will send you to someone else who will. But I see now that I was not supposed to go to Tulane. From a spiritual perspective, I know that God allowed me to go to Delaware for his purposes and his sovereign reasons, which eventually led me to Liberty University.

Pharaoh told Moses he would let the children of Israel go, and then he changed his mind and began pursuing them with chariots and trying to kill them. The end result for the pharaoh was an army that drowned in the Red Sea. When God protects you, no other protection is needed. So it was with my coach at Delaware. After letting me go and coming after me with slanderous character insults, and after his short-lived success at UD, no one heard from him for quite some time within the coaching arena. The University of Delaware had fired him—which would not have been normal after going to the NCAA tournament for two seasons in a row. After getting fired, he was last seen working at a community college somewhere in Delaware, which I know was humbling for him. The UD athletic director said that they felt he was getting too big for his britches, and they had to get rid of him. They also said that he could not find a coaching job anywhere because nobody wanted him. I don't know where he is today, or what he is doing, but I hope and pray that he ended up giving his heart to Jesus Christ. God gave him a personal confirmation of his presence and power that would leave the coach without any excuse. That confirmation was me.

Sent on Assignment

I took out a loan and applied for financial aid for the rest of that first semester at Liberty, and I began classes and went to practice with the team. I was not officially on the team when I first arrived, and had to try out, so to speak, as I was under a close watch. I was not worried because I knew that God sent me to Liberty and that he did not bring me this far to leave me. I was a Division I basketball player who also knew his ability to play basketball. Besides, there was nowhere else for me to go because I was not going back home and I certainly wasn't going back to Delaware. I attended classes every day, practiced with the team, and worked hard. When the team went on the road I stayed on campus and continued going to my classes, but I was allowed to sit on the bench during home games.

I used to enjoy the pre-game chapels we would have in the locker room before entering the arena. I especially enjoyed Dr. Falwell's talks, as he was such a powerful and motivating speaker. After his pre-game devotions I always felt like I could do anything in my life with the help of Jesus. This all was a little weird to me because I had just left a scholarship at UD, took out a loan, got financial aid, and enrolled at LU for an opportunity to attend a Christian university and try out for a Christian university basketball team. The weird part was that I was enjoying every bit of this new and better experience. My new teammates were such a great group of guys, and I had the privilege of playing with one of my good friends, Liberty's center at the time, Julius "Juice" Nuwasu, who went on to play for the NBA's San Antonio Spurs. I knew that I was sent on an assignment by God.

Liberty was a life changing experience and one of the best things that ever happened to me—after salvation and marrying my beautiful wife (who I met there). Liberty was a solace for me. Here was a university where just about everyone was wearing Christian T-shirts and outwardly professing their faith in Jesus Christ. I fit right in. There were so many resources available for Christian growth, and I took advantage of them all. We had chapel three times a week, and there were conferences, Christian concerts, mid-week Bible study, church services on Sunday mornings and Sunday nights—and I was at every one of them. And even though I could not sing, I joined the fellowship choir. I just wanted to praise the Lord for the great things he had done. I felt like I was on a retreat every day.

Of course not every student on campus was totally sold out for Christ, but a great percentage were. I made Christian friendships that will last a lifetime, including meeting my best friend, my beautiful wife, Nikki, who is a great woman of God. The icing on the cake was when Dr. Jerry Falwell and the Liberty coaches decided to give me a scholarship my redshirt junior year after sitting out the first five games of the season. That would conclude sitting out a year due to NCAA regulations. The Lord had restored the opportunity for me not only to play college basketball, but to play for God's team, the Liberty University Flames.

He Adds No Sorrow with It

The next season, during my redshirt junior year, our team went on to make NCAA history as the first Christian institution to ever play in the Final 64s March Madness. We beat Coastal Carolina in Charleston, South Carolina, to win the Big South tournament. It was awesome to see all the faithful Liberty students make their way down to the coliseum to support the Flames. Our students were so enthusiastic and loud that you would have thought we were in the Vines Center in Lynchburg. After winning this hard fought game, our team, the students, and the coaches flooded the floor to celebrate our victory. The team lifted Dr. Jerry Falwell on their shoulders above the crowd. He was one of the kindest men I had ever met, and he did not care about us ruining his tailor made suit. He really loved the university and he really loved the kids. He then went up the ladder during the net cutting ceremony and cut down his piece of the net. We cheered as he turned around and waved at all of us while displaying his signature smile. This was a big win for us, and the students poured onto the LU campus with toilet paper in celebration. Just because we were Christians did not mean we could not have clean fun.

We later found out the Flames would be the sixteenth seed in the east region of the tournament. This meant we would play against the number one seeded and nationally ranked powerhouse: the North Carolina Tar Heels. They had a number of former NBA players, including Eric Montross, Kevin Salvadori, Jerry Stackhouse, Donte Calabria, and Derrick Phelps. They also had Rasheed Wallace, my good friend from Philadelphia. What was such a blessing about playing in the east region of the tournament was that we got the opportunity to play in the US Airways Arena in Washington, D.C., where the NBA's Washington Wizards played. So our family and friends got to join with those watching around the country to see us play live. We lost the game, but surprisingly as the sixteenth seed we were winning 51 to 50 at half time. The newspapers already had their headlines ready as it seemed like it was going to be a "David beats Goliath" story. But on that day Goliath won against David. After that game the nation knew something about this small Christian school in Lynchburg, Virginia.

My dream of being a Christian athlete who excelled at basketball on the Division I level had finally come true. I was a reserve player, but it was still an awesome experience because now I felt like I was a part of something bigger than me. I was so thankful to know that my gifts, talents, abilities, and faith were being cultivated and embraced. That was all I ever wanted at Delaware. The Lord granted me some of the greatest memories of my life by sending me to Liberty University. God restored what I thought I lost by walking away from the University of Delaware, and he gave it right back to me—this time better than before. When God blesses you, sorrow will be nowhere in the equation. As Proverbs 10:22 says, "The blessings of the Lord makes one rich, and He adds no sorrow with it."

At the beginning of my redshirt senior year I had just arrived on campus and was going through a very stressful check-in process. I got so frustrated that I had to go back to my dorm to take a nap. After waking up and continuing on with the check-in process, I was standing in line in the Vines Center, where we played our basketball games, preparing to get my books for the semester. A young man and a young lady introduced themselves to me. The lady's name was Legia, and she asked me if I would be interested in playing professionally in Europe after my senior season was over. I did not hesitate to say, "I sure would." She told me to call her friend Armenio Anjos, a Portuguese Christian agent, after my season was over. She also told me she had been watching my testimony around campus the last year or so and finally decided to approach me. I had mixed feelings about this because I was happy the Lord allowed me to uphold a good testimony, but on the other hand I could not help but think about the blessings I had forfeited—especially when I was at the University of Delaware going through phases of my relationship that involved sin. God has people everywhere, and you never know who is around you and watching you, especially as it relates to your testimony. What I learned in this circumstance was that upholding a good consistent testimony can sometimes not only open up doors but fulfill dreams as well.

We had a winning season my senior year, but we did not earn our way back to the NCAA tournament. Coastal Carolina dropped out of the Big South conference, and that left our conference with eleven teams instead of twelve. According to NCAA guidelines, in order for any team to earn an automatic bid to the March Madness tournament, it must have a minimum of twelve teams in its conference altogether. The team that wins their conference championship gets to go to the "Big Dance." The only other way to be invited into the national field of sixty-four teams was to win a convincing number of games so that the NCAA committee would invite the team in. This was the case with our team this particular year. In order for us to have made it back we would have had to earn our way by practically winning every game—something that is not impossible, but a very tough thing to do. This year, Liberty University's campus hosted the Big South tournament. Our campus got selected because of our beautiful arena that seated ten thousand people easily. We ended up losing in the second round of the tournament. Even in a losing effort, I was proud of our team and proud of myself because in every game I left everything out there on the floor. In fact, after the game was over, I fell on the floor face down and just laid there for a minute or two. I could not believe that my college career was over.

After the season was over, my roommate and good friend, Jason Dixon, and I got invited to play in a post season, pro prospect tournament in Billings, Montana. Jason, who eventually went on to play professionally, and I were on the same team. I made sure I passed him the ball because I wanted to see him do well. I played some of the best basketball of my life and could attribute a lot of it being used to the open court style of play from my early days in the Philadelphia Public and Sony Hill leagues. To be able to play without any restrictions was right up my alley because that was the way I tended to excel. I played very well in the four games we played that weekend. I averaged twenty points a game, but the most amazing stat was that I only missed three shots during the tournament. I had to make sure I got a copy of the stats to prove what I did and to keep for the memories.

Ball in Portugal

Back at Liberty after the tournament, I gave Armenio Anjos a call at his home in Portugal. He asked me to send some stats from my senior season at Liberty, along with a tape of one of my best games. I sent a tape of a preseason game where I scored twenty-five points in a scrimmage against the Finland National Team. My concern was my senior season stats because, even though I started, the role my coaches gave me was to throw the ball inside to Jason and Peter first, who were 6'10" and 6'11" respectively. Being obedient to my coaches and my role, I only averaged 7.3 points per game. I was competing for an overseas job with college players from all around the country who averaged two or even three times as many points as I did, and who went to bigger and better-known schools as well. Because of this, I also sent the stats from the post season pro prospect tournament I had just played where I averaged twenty points per game and where I missed only three shots the whole tournament.

In seeking God and asking for wisdom and direction in the situation, I felt he, in his infinite wisdom, impressed on my heart that I should write and ask for the opportunity to play in Portugal. I decided to humble myself and pour out my heart. In the letter to Armenio, I said, “Judging from my Liberty University stats you could be tempted to think that this letter is a waste of your time. However, please look at the tape and the post senior season tournament stats. I think you will see that I have the talent and the ability to play on a professional level. The reason I only averaged 7.3 points per game was because of the role my coaches gave me, and I humbly accepted it for the best interest of our team. I’m asking for an opportunity to get in the door—I’ll do the rest. Thank you for your time and consideration in this matter, and I look forward to hearing from you soon.”

My basketball season ended in March, and six months later I got a call from Armenio saying he got me a tryout with a team in Portugal called FISICA. This tryout routine was starting to become a trend. He told me to pack my clothes for one week because that was the amount of time the team would need to evaluate me. I told Armenio, “I’m packing my clothes for the entire season because I’m not coming back until after the season is over!” I knew by faith I would make the team.

My first game was an exhibition game, and we played against a team called Immortal, the best one in our division. They had an NBA-caliber player who played for the

Brazilian National Team at one point, named Fabio. He was 6'9" and could handle the ball and score from anywhere on the floor. At 6'7" I had to guard him, but that was okay with me because he had to guard me, too. The game became a shoot-out as he scored forty-two points on me and I scored thirty-six on him. We both tried to defend one another as best we could, but in that game our shooting was just that superb. Our team upset them, and that was a big win because that was the first time FISICA beat that team in the history of Portuguese basketball. It may have been only an exhibition game, but not to our guys. We celebrated like we had won the championship.

My tryout week went very well with my performance and our win. I already knew I was going to make the team because God told me to pack my clothes for the entire season, and by faith I did. I also knew that God did not bring me this far to leave me. To make a long story short, I did make the team, I averaged 30.3 points a game for the season, and I was selected MVP of our league. I was able to bring my dad over to Portugal to see me play professionally, and that was a dream come true for both of us.

Cultivating for Ministry

God also used my time in Portugal to really mold me as a future youth pastor. Every day I hung out with the Portuguese kids because they were the only English speakers in the neighborhood. They learned English in school, and the chance to talk to me was an opportunity for them to continue practicing and learning. They showed me everything—how to count the money, where to go shopping, even where the arcade and movies were. The kids and I did just about everything together. It was a little embarrassing to have kids knock on my door and say, "Mr. Ken, can you come out and play today?" I would say, "Okay, I'll be right out." We had a lot of fun going rollerblading, hiking, skate boarding, to the movies, and to the arcade. I even had all the neighborhood kids come over my house to watch *Terminator 2: Judgment Day*. It was this experience that taught me how to relate to youth and speak their language, which helps me minister to young people better today. The impact of the kids on me was so great that I am still a big kid at heart to this very day, and I think I always will be. My best friend, Paulo, was a true blessing because during the times I got a little homesick, he and his family were a great support to me and helped me adjust to a whole new country and culture. I was blessed for the opportunity to lead Paulo to the Lord one day while we went for a walk, and I gave him the same little green Gideon Bible that the unknown man gave me when I went for a walk that night at the University of Delaware.

I also met another missionary family who took me in, and they were a blessing as well. They were from the United States, but they lived in the town where I played. After one of my games, we had an opportunity to talk, and they invited me over to their house for dinner. They were so warm and welcoming and showed me so much love and acceptance. What made this even more significant was that they were a caucasian family. I am not saying this to focus on race because God is about grace and not race. My coach at the University of Delaware was caucasian, and he had rejected me so completely that I anticipated most caucasian people would do the same thing. But the love of Christ this family showed me brought healing in my life. Their little son loved me, too, and after we would eat and fellowship with the family, we would play video games for the rest of the day until it was time to leave. The family even took me to church on Sundays, to a church they had started in the town. It was awesome, even though I could not understand the language. What I did understand was the atmosphere of worship and the sound of the name Jesus. To watch Portuguese people worshiping God as passionately as we do in America was awe inspiring. I learned that God can use all our experiences to cultivate us for ministry. He will send people into our lives to impact us so we can have an impact on others and the kingdom of Christ

76ers Camp

After playing in Portugal, I was invited to the 76ers rookie and free agent camp, which was held at the Community College of Philadelphia in the summer of 1996. The camp was being run by Maurice Cheeks, a former 76er, and his scouting staff. I played extremely well the first day of camp and it seemed I could not miss. In fact, I literally did not miss a shot the first day of camp. I found out later that my mother was lifting me up in prayer during those specific hours. Everyone wanted to guard me to try to stop me. They said, "I got him, let me guard him, I got him." I played so well that Maurice Cheeks invited me back the next day when the veterans would be there. Some notable

NBA players participating in the veterans camp included my friends Jerome Allen of the Minnesota Timber Wolves, Paul "Snoop" Graham of the Atlanta Hawks, and Shawn Harvey of the Dallas Mavericks. Some other notable NBA players at camp were Rick Mahorn of the Detroit Pistons, Kobe Bryant, who eventually ended up with the Los Angeles Lakers, and many more players. I had the privilege of guarding Kobe Bryant during some pickup games. After the camp was over, I walked up to Kobe and said, "Hey man, God bless you," and extended my hand to shake his. He returned the favor and humbly responded, "Thank you very much." I did that not only because I was impressed with his obvious ability, but a lot of players were talking trash to Kobe. But after I saw what he could do, I said to myself, "That young boy can play—I don't care what anybody says." I have never been surprised at what he has accomplished throughout his NBA career.

In the end I did not make the 76ers team but I was proud to have given it a chance. I played well and gained the respect of a lot of NBA players, scouts, and coaches. When the NBA players had closed workouts at Drexel, Temple, La Salle, Germantown Friends School, and the Bellevue Club in Center City Philadelphia, I got the call to come and play. It was because the players knew I could play on their level. Even though I did not make it to the NBA, this experience gave me closure about wondering if I could really do it. I knew I could because I was out there with them, and I was doing it. The Lord blessed me to play basketball professionally for two more years—one year in Taiwan, China, and another in mainland, China.

My Destiny in Jesus Christ's Perfect Plan

Later that same summer after the 76ers camp and before playing my first season in Asia, I was invited to play with Christian basketball organizations like Athletes in Action and the Christ Crusaders. We traveled to countries like Brazil to play friendly exhibition games and, more importantly, to share our faith. The most exciting trip was when we went to China to tour with the China National Team for exhibition games in the major cities. To play in one city we had to sail across the Yangtze River, the third largest river in the world. We had police escorts and mobs of people showing up in every city to see us and their homeland team, as well. Our main objective was to represent Christ on and off the court, and to try witnessing to the team with our conduct (since there was a language barrier). Of course, in China we had more strict guidelines for straightforward evangelism, but we did manage to give each player a Bible as a gift with personal letters from each player inside of them. At that time, Wang Zhi-Zhi, the first Chinese athlete to ever play in the NBA, was on the China National Team. Other NBA players on the China National Team were Ma'nek Ba'tier of the San Antonio Spurs, and 7'2" Yoa Ming of the Houston Rockets.

During my season in Taiwan, China, the league was very competitive, and it was run just like the NBA. We had Upper Deck rookie cards and sneaker endorsement contracts and everything. I had so many free pairs of sneakers that I left about fifteen pairs in my apartment upon returning to the United States. I just could not fit all of them in my suitcases. I had so much basketball equipment. When

I would return to the United States, I would stop off in California and stay with my brother David, who was the recreation director for Orange County. I would put on free clinics for the kids and give away shorts, socks, T-shirts, and other equipment, just to get rid of them and encourage the kids. I would also put on dunking exhibitions, and my brother was so proud of me.

My coach in Taiwan was an awesome Christian. We got along very well and became good friends. He and I would secretly go to the Chinese underground church for worship services on Sundays. This was an eye-opening and life changing experience, because the Chinese people were not allowed to worship God publicly. Yet they had a passion for the Lord I had never seen in America. It was almost as if they worshiped God like it was their last service. I later found out that if the underground church had been discovered, it would have been their last worship service. The people worshiped Jesus as if he was right in the room. Even though they spoke in the Mandarin language, I recognized *Yasu*, which means *Jesus*. Experiencing Chinese worship made me feel ashamed about the lackadaisical praise and worship we sometimes give the Lord in our country. Maybe if we were under the same life-threatening social pressures the Chinese Christians were under, we would worship the Lord more passionately, too.

I also had the opportunity to meet my favorite martial artist, actor, and action hero, Jackie Chan, at our League Christmas party. At the party they had a fifty foot Christmas tree made out of basketballs spiraling from the bottom all the way to the top. Jackie Chan was the honorary guest who was hoisted to the top of the Christmas tree with a crane in order to put the star basketball on top of it. He was very nice as he posed, took pictures, and signed autographs for everybody. I got the chance to get his autograph on the back of the paper plate I had just finished eating my food on. After that, I reached out my hand to shake his hand and the local Taiwanese newspaper snapped a picture of us shaking hands. The picture was put on the front cover of the newspaper and the sports page. I still have the picture and will keep it forever.

Nikki and Full-Time Ministry

When my season in Taiwan was over, I married my college sweetheart and best friend, Nikki, who has been the love of my life. After our honeymoon we headed to mainland China, where I would play my final professional basketball season. It was great having my number one cheerleader cheering for me during every game. After this season was over, God began to move us in another direction—one that involved ministry to children, youth, teens, young adults, men, and senior citizens on a megachurch level. God called me into full-time ministry as a recreational director, youth and young adult pastor, and an associate minister called to preach the good news of Jesus Christ.

I have felt more fulfilled in my life doing ministry and complying with my lifelong God-given assignment than I did playing basketball on any level. All the points I scored, the awards I won, the places I traveled, the money I made, and all the amazing people I have met along the way cannot compare to the sense of contentment and wholeness I feel doing God's work. Even when compared to a seemingly disappointing college career and not making it to the NBA, I finally gained a perspective that brought me a level of resolve in connection with my dreams and true purpose for living. As Paul said, "Yet indeed I also count all things loss for the excellence of the knowledge of Christ Jesus my Lord, for whom I have suffered the loss of all things, and count them as rubbish, that I may gain Christ" (Phil. 3:8). I finally learned and accepted that being where God wanted me and doing what he wanted me to do allowed me to find true satisfaction. The time I spent chasing a dream outside of his direct will led to a journey of constantly searching for significance but never truly finding it. That has since changed because I have found my destiny in Jesus Christ's perfect plan for me. God is in total control, and even the things we think we have lost, or the moves we think are detours and road blocks are part of his sovereign plan over our lives.

I am still trying to lead people to the saving grace and knowledge of the Lord, just as I did when I was trying to share the gospel with my teammates and coaches back in college. Maybe I'll be known among the long list of great players the NBA has never seen, and maybe not. Whatever the case, I know that it was not because I did not have the talent and ability. While attending an NBA game in Philadelphia, a friend of my dad told him, "There is a reason why Kevin is not out there." Many years later I learned that it was because God had another plan for my life—a plan that would involve impacting the world in different way. That plan entails telling people about a loving God who wants to have a personal relationship with them here and now. And it also entails warning people about the consequences of rejecting Christ's free gift of salvation. Hell is a very real place, and we are going to take a field trip there. But before we do, let's think about some of the most frequently asked questions about it.

CHAPTER FOUR

Let's Bring Some Clarity: the God of Balance

The first concept most of us learned about God concerned his unfathomable love and forgiveness. He delights in and is eager to extend his grace and mercy to all. If the world outside of the church knows nothing else about God, it knows that he is love. The apostle Paul wrote, "Yet in all these things we are more than conquerors through Him that loved us. For I am persuaded that neither death nor life, nor angels nor principalities nor powers, nor things present nor things to come, nor height, nor depth, nor any other created thing, shall be able to separate us from the love of God which is in Christ Jesus our Lord" (Rom. 8:37-39). Therefore, the concept of God creating hell and sending anyone to such a place is hard to accept.

Indeed, nothing can separate us from the love of God, not even hell. When we were children and disobeyed our parents, they disciplined us. Even though they meted out punishment, they never stopped loving us. In fact, when they told us our punishment hurt them more than it did us, that was probably true. They did it for our own good. They warned us about our choices and behavior time and time again before reaching a decision to discipline us. Our parent's warnings were given to us so that we could take advantage of the opportunity to choose to change our direction. This was how we learned the very important biblical principle of God's love and forgiveness.

The principle of God's love and forgiveness is similar. He will forgive all who ask for forgiveness in sincerity, but even with his forgiveness there are still consequences for our bad choices and sin. God is our heavenly parent, and he gets no pleasure in sending anyone to hell. There are consequences, however, for rejecting Jesus Christ and dying in a state of unbelief. Just like our parents did, God in his grace and mercy gives us numerous warnings beforehand about our choices. We can take advantage of these warnings by choosing to change directions.

There is no sense in which God bullies anyone into accepting Jesus. Actually, it is the total opposite. God loves us so much he wants to rescue us from the brink, change us progressively over time, use us to impact a dark and dying world for his kingdom, and, when this life is over, spend eternity in heaven with us. The penalty of hell for rejecting Christ is because Jesus, God's only begotten Son, demonstrated his love toward us by paying a very heavy price on the cross—by dying for our sins and the sins of the world. That kind of divine love should compel us to want to give our lives to Christ, to live for him and serve him, and to feel forever indebted to him. God wants us to give him our hearts willingly because of his charity, not because of the consequences of hell.

God of Love, God of Wrath

The gospel of Matthew records Jesus saying "And do not fear those who kill the body but cannot kill the soul. But rather fear Him who is able to destroy both soul and body in Hell" (10:28). And in Luke 12:5, Jesus says, "But I will show you whom you should fear: Fear Him who, after He has killed, has power to cast into Hell; yes, I say to you, fear Him!" Are we to fear this God who loves us and forgives us? Is this the same God we are told we can never be separated from? The answer is yes, because while God is a God of love, he is also a God of wrath. He is a God of stability and balance, of the mountaintop experience and the valley, and of blessings and curses. In short, he is the God of heaven as well as hell.

Flowers need a balance of sunshine and rain to grow and mature. If a plant gets too much sunshine and not enough rain, it can die. And if a plant gets too much rain and not enough sunshine, it can die as well. It is the balance of both sunshine and rain that keeps the flowers growing healthy and strong. God does the same with us as his children, for it is the balance of joy and pain that he allows in our lives that keeps us growing spiritually healthy and strong. There is one key ingredient, however, that determines if we grow spiritually or slowly deteriorate spiritually over time. That ingredient is our choice of what kind of attitude we will have with the pain we experience in life. John Maxwell once said that life is ten percent what happens to you and ninety percent how you respond. James, the brother of Jesus, wrote that you should "count it all joy when you fall into various trails, knowing that the testing of your faith produces patience. But let patience have her perfect work, that you may be perfect and complete, lacking nothing" (James 1:2-4). The attitude of counting it all joy, through happiness and sorrow, makes us better instead of bitter. This is evidence in our lives that God is a God of balance.

Being perfect, complete, and lacking nothing means that God has a measure of maturity he wants us to discover from the trials we face. Our tests of faith prepare us for the next levels of maturity, and without them we are incomplete or lacking in spiritual development. This is not to say there is any failure in God because there is no failure in God. It is just that without taking our lessons from our trials, we end up having to go through those same tests of faith all over again. Through the strength and power of the Holy Spirit, and by keeping a good attitude, we endure to the end. The reason we can have hope in our trails is because God is a God of balance. We can be encouraged while going through painful situations because we know they will eventually come to an end. "For His anger is but for a moment, His favor is for life: Weeping may endure for a night, But joy comes in the morning" (Ps. 30:5).

The balance of good and bad, ups and downs, joy and pain allowed by God in our lives matures us into who we become. In the end we become more like Jesus Christ and draw closer to him in the process. As the letter to the Romans states, "And not only that, but we also glory in tribulations, knowing that tribulation produces perseverance; perseverance, character; and character, hope. Now hope does not disappoint us, because the love of God has been poured out into our hearts by the Holy Spirit, who was given to us" (Rom. 5:3-5). Again, God is a God of balance.

I must admit that the God of balance can be very unfair at times. This is especially true when he is showering us with blessings. The love, grace, and mercy we have already received from God is not fair, and we don't deserve it. Not to mention the love, grace, and mercy we continue receiving on a daily basis. "For His anger is but for a moment, His favor is for life" (Ps. 30:5). God is a God of balance, but when it comes to his love, grace, and mercy towards us, he wants to be unfair. This is what makes him the incomprehensible loving God to whom we should want to willingly give our hearts and lives.

Job

When we look at the life of Job in the Old Testament we are tempted to think that God was being unfair in allowing all the horrible things to happen in Job's life. After all, Job suffered more than anyone else in the entire Bible (aside from Jesus), and God allowed it all to occur. To make matters worse, Job was blameless, upright, God-fearing, and he shunned evil. Why then did he lose so much—all in the same day? (1:13-19; 2:7-8). His oxen and donkeys were stolen and his servants were killed. His sheep got burned up and more of his servants were killed. His camels were stolen by the Chaldeans, and more servants were killed. His seven sons and three daughters were all killed when a house collapsed. Satan struck him with painful boils from the soles of his feet to the crown of his head. He had to take a pottery fragment to scrape himself while he sat on ashes.

All of this happened to a man God himself called faultless. Was this deserved? Was it fair and balanced? God is unfair when he is showering us with many blessings. And he can be just as unfair when he is restoring. We see that at the end of Job's life story, after he prayed for his three friends, Eliphaz the Temanite, Bildad the Shuhite, and Zophar the Naamathite, he received his double portion of fourteen thousand sheep, six thousand camels, one thousand yoke of oxen, and one thousand female donkeys. He also had seven sons and three daughters. "And the Lord restored Job's losses when he prayed for his friends. Indeed the Lord gave Job twice as much as he had before…The Lord blessed the latter part of Job's life more than the first" (42:10; 12-13).

God is the God of balance. Even though he may sometimes ask something of us that requires faith, when he chooses to be imbalanced it is when he is blessing us. When God does this it is because of his love, grace, and mercy that we come out blessed, despite whatever pain and suffering we endure. That is what makes him God.

The Righteous Judge

God is also a righteous judge. "For I proclaim the name of the Lord: Ascribe greatness to our God. He is the Rock, His work is perfect; For all His ways are justice, A God of truth and without injustice, Righteous and upright is He" (Deut. 32:3-4). The word *just* is a derivative of the word justice, and a God who hates injustice is always fair and just.

This Scripture describes God in terms of his work being perfect, his ways being just, a God of truth, without injustice of any kind, and one who is righteous and upright. If this is true, how does allowing people to go to hell fall in line with a perfect work and with a righteous and upright God? How does allowing people to go to hell square with God always being just? The answer is the heavy price the Son of God paid for our salvation. That salvation is a gift to all, and we choose either it or damnation. There is nothing in between. God gives us the choice to choose whatever we want to do in life, but we are not able to choose the consequences. This is because of the law of the harvest—a principle that God has set in order. That law says that we will eventually reap what we sow. We are told this in the book of Galatians, which says, "Do not be deceived, God is not mocked; for whatever a man sows, that he will also reap" (6:7). For example, if a person has been summoned by a judge to appear in court on a certain date for breaking the law, they have the choice to go or not. The consequences of not going might be a sentence to time in jail. The law breaker is not able to choose the consequences. This means God does not send anyone to hell, but rather that people choose hell themselves. The Righteous Judge only executes judgment based on the choices we make. When a judge sentences a criminal to jail, he or she is not doing it because they are just trying to be mean. They do it because they are obligated to execute right judgment in connection to the law. The criminals themselves chose to break the law, and it was their decision putting them in the position of serving time. In that same way God also executes right judgment based on his law, which is his Word.

The term *judge* has two meanings. The first is to pronounce sentence, as in lawgiving or executing judgment. Examples of this meaning would include God judging Sodom and Gomorrah, (Gen. 18:25), God delivering someone (1 Sam. 24:18), or God vindicating a person (Ps. 10:18).

The second meaning of the word *judge* has to do with a legal context—being put in jail or going to court. The implication is an unfavorable verdict leading to punishment. Condemning and punishing might be the way in which judgment is carried out by God. One's reaction to faith in Christ is going to determine how he will judge, whether heaven or hell. Another example of the second meaning of the word *judge* would include the judgment a person passes on another person in condemnation.

A Courtroom Drama

In Scripture, *to judge* is used mostly in connection with God's judgment on humanity. Think of the story of Adam and Eve: God is the Righteous Judge in a courtroom with Adam and Eve, who are representing humankind. Satan, the accuser, is in charge of the prosecution. The charge against Adam and Eve, the defendants, is disobeying and rebelling against God. After the serpent deceived Eve into eating the forbidden fruit from the tree of the knowledge of good and evil, she gave it to her husband. God then kicked them out of the Garden of Eden and delivered a subpoena for them to appear in penalty court. The plaintiffs were death, hell, and the grave, all represented by Satan. The Word of God was the jury.

As God, the Righteous Judge, walked in the courtroom with fire in his eyes, the two angels who secured the courtroom announced, "All rise, the Honorable Judge God the

Father presiding. Court is now in session." Once God the Father had taken his seat, one of the angels securing the courtroom said, "You may be seated." Satan, representing death, hell, and the grave went first, as he began stating his case against the obviously guilty Adam and Eve.

Satan's opening argument was a crushing one for the defendants, as he appealed to the Judge by saying, "Your Honor, did you not say you are not a man that you should lie?" (Num. 23:19). "And did you not say that you had the name that was above all other names?" (Phil. 2:9). "Furthermore, did you not say that you exalted your name and your word above all things (Ps. 138:2) and that it would never come back to you void?" (Isa. 55:11). Satan tried to secure the victory with his closing argument. "Lastly, Your Honor, did you not say that without the shedding of blood there is no forgiveness of sin?" (Heb. 9:22). With this the prosecutor rested his case and grinned as he took his seat.

God is a just and Righteous Judge who has to render a fair decision based on his character. He must execute judgment, for it would be going against his nature not to do so. Because all the evidence points to their guilt, Adam and Eve are sure to be found guilty, and an unfavorable verdict is going to be rendered leading to punishment. Based on their being deceived by the accuser, they will be sentenced to hell, and the rest of humankind with them. Unless some kind of a miracle takes place, hell is where they are heading.

The courtroom was totally silent as they waited for the verdict that Judge God the Father would render. The Judge turned toward Adam and Even with an angry look on his face because Satan presented what appeared to be a flawless case. Adam and Eve were sweating profusely because it did not look good for them or mankind, as God was just about to speak.

But before the Judge even asked Adam and Eve to state their case, the courtroom doors flew open and a Lawyer (who has never lost a case) walked in with three witnesses: goodness, grace, and mercy. Excitement filled the courtroom as he approached the bench. Facing the Judge on the same side as Adam and Eve, the young Lawyer said, "I'm their Lawyer and Defense Attorney, and I'll speak on their behalf." He then turned towards Adam and Eve and said, "I may not come when you want me to, but I'll be right on time." Judge God the Father said, "State your name, Sir." Goodness, grace, and mercy, standing in front of the Judge, responded for him in unison, "His name is Jesus, and he is the Son of the Living God who came to take away the sin of the world" (John 1:29). Jesus stepped forward and showed his nail-scarred hands and feet and his pierced side. He settled the case by saying, "Father, forgive them for they know not what they do" (Luke. 23:34).

The Judge then reached his decision and said, "Because of the indisputable evidence that God so loved the World that he gave his only begotten Son, that whosoever believeth in him shall not perish, but have everlasting life (John 3:16), I am throwing out the case. Satan, your case is dismissed." God slammed down the gavel and said, "Court is adjourned." Jesus won the case and Adam and Eve, along with humankind, received an undeserved second chance. Upon leaving the courtroom, the prosecutor said, "This is not over yet. I'll be back," and began laughing as he and his support team exited the courtroom.

Declared Righteous

The price Jesus paid for the forgiveness of our sins and our redemption was a very high one. It cost him his life. The blood he shed on Calvary's cross was an atoning sacrifice and, as a result, we are declared righteous. This does not mean we are righteous, but we are now in right standing with God again. The vindication we received means this forgiveness was not something we had but rather something that we needed—and God gave it to us. Now when God looks at us he sees Jesus' righteousness and, as a result, he sees us just as if we had never sinned. This should put a premium on our decision to escape the deserved penalty of hell by accepting Christ in our hearts as Lord and Savior.

God is a God of balance and he is fair and just. He does not desire that anyone spend eternity in hell; what he wants is for everyone to spend eternity with him in heaven. "The Lord is not slack concerning His promise, as some men count slackness, but is longsuffering toward us, not willing that any should perish, but that all should come to repentance. But the day of the Lord will come as a thief in the night, in which the heavens will pass away with great noise, and the elements will melt with fervent heat; both the earth and the works that are in it will be burned up" (2 Pet. 3:9-10).

Unfortunately, not everyone is going to heaven. This is because of the choices people will make not to accept Jesus as the perfect sacrifice for sin, and the Lord and Savior of humankind. Because of hardened hearts, many, many will refuse to surrender and repent. On Judgment Day, God will face his creation with either fire or fondness in his eyes. Will we face the Creator as punisher or pardoner? As condemner or comforter? This all depends on us, for the choice is ours.

CHAPTER FIVE

God's Original Design: A Place Not Meant for Us

At some undetermined point after God created the heavens and the earth and the earth being formless and empty—between the first and second verses of Genesis—Lucifer coveted the power and glory of Almighty God and tried to usurp divine authority. Lucifer was created by God as one of the mightiest angels in the entire angelic host. Lucifer's job was to reflect the glory of God back to God; in fact, his name actually meant "light bearer." Lucifer was also in charge of the music that played in front of the Lord's throne. (Even in his fallen state today he still has influence over music, and that is why we need to be very careful about what kinds of music we listen to.) Because of his pride and covetousness and his desire to be like the Most High, Lucifer decided to keep the glory for himself instead of reflecting it back to the Creator. In essence, Lucifer was saying he was incomplete—a bad creation made by a bad Creator. He was the originator of the term "wannabe," because he wanted to be like the Most High God. "How you are fallen from heaven, O Lucifer, son of the morning! How you are cut down to the ground, you who weakened the nations! For you have said in your heart: 'I will ascend into heaven, I will exalt my throne above the stars of God; I will also sit on the mount of the congregation on the farthest sides of the north; I will ascend above the heights of the clouds, I will be like the Most High.' Yet you shall be brought down to Sheol, to the lowest depths of the Pit" (Isa. 14:12-15).

When we covet the lives of others, we are offending God by saying in effect "God, I don't want to be the unique person that you created me to be." Instead, we are saying that we don't want the perfect plan God has for our lives because we want to be like someone else. We are not satisfied with the good thing that God created us to be. Along with our desire to be what God did not create us to be, we, like Lucifer, are not only calling ourselves a bad creation of God but also calling God a bad Creator.

Satan is no match for God and he knows it. The rebellion in heaven was not only of Lucifer, but also of one third of the other angels, who he deceived and who are now fallen angels. The book of Revelation says: "His tail drew a third of the stars of heaven and threw them to the earth…And war broke out in heaven: Michael and his angels fought with the dragon; and the dragon and his angels fought, but they did not prevail, nor was a place found for them in heaven any longer. So the great dragon was cast out, that serpent of old, called the Devil and Satan, who deceives the whole world; he was cast to the earth, and his angels were cast out with him" (12:4, 7-9).

Misconceptions About the Fall of Satan

There are misconceptions about the fall of Satan and the heavenly war that broke out afterwards. There was no one-on-one challenge between Lucifer and God. How could there have been? Lucifer is no match for God; the opposite of Satan is the archangel Michael, not God. The war that broke out caused a struggle between Satan and his fallen army and Michael, the archangel, and his angelic host. There was no struggle for God to kick Satan out of heaven. Luke 10:18 says: "And He said to them, I saw Satan fall like lightning from heaven." This Scripture does not sound like God had a struggle evicting Satan from the heavenly realm.

If Satan knew he could not overthrow God, why did he rebel in the first place and bring consequences on himself and the angels who followed him? The answer is *sin*. Sin looks and feels good for a season, and then after that it requires a debt payback with interest called consequences. Ultimately, Michael and his fierce army called on the name of the Lord and rebuked Satan in God's name, defeating him and his fallen followers. Earlier, Michael defeated Satan in another battle when they were both contending for the body of Moses. In that battle as well he called on the name of the Lord to rebuke Satan (Jude 9).

And here is the answer to our first question of where hell came from. In God's original design, hell was created for Satan and his fallen angels due to their heavenly rebellion. It was never meant for humans. The gospel of Matthew says, "Then He will also say to those on the left hand, 'Depart from Me, you cursed, into the everlasting fire prepared for the devil and his angels'" (25:41). How is hell identified in Scripture? Here are some of the names:

- *Hell (Ps. 55:19)*
- *Hades (Luke. 16:23)*
- *Sheol (Job 17:16)*

- *Everlasting fire (Matt. 25:41)*
- *Everlasting punishment (Matt. 25:46)*
- *The bottomless pit (Rev. 20:3)*
- *The pit (Num. 16:33)*
- *Furnace of fire (Matt. 13:42)*
- *The Great furnace (Rev. 9:2)*
- *Eternal fire (Jude 1:7)*
- *Lake of fire (Rev. 20:9)*
- *Great gulf (Luke 16:26)*
- *Outer darkness (Matt. 8:12)*
- *The lake which burns with fire and brimstone (Rev. 21:8)*
- *Everlasting destruction (2 Thess. 1:9)*
- *Hell fire (Matt 18:9)*

The Keys to Hades, the Grave, and Death

The fall of the original humans, Adam and Eve, brought sin into our world. This sin gave us another possible destination besides heaven: hell. But the death, burial, and resurrection of Jesus Christ have redeemed humankind from the deserved penalty of hell. Once the keys to Hades, the grave, and death were held by Satan, but now they are held by Jesus. From all the way back to Adam and Eve, Satan has tried to thwart and stop the plan of God. But he did not succeed. Jesus fulfilled the prophecy that the Messiah would rise again three days after death. Mathew 12:40

says, "For as Jonah was three days and three nights in the belly of the great fish, so will the Son of Man be three days and three nights in the heart of the earth." To those who demanded a miraculous sign, Jesus answered, "Destroy this temple, and in three days I will raise it up." (John 2:19). The game has now changed, for Jesus has defeated Satan and death itself.

The book of Revelation says, "I *am* He who lives, and was dead, and behold, I am alive forevermore. Amen. And I have the keys of Hades and of Death" (1:18). Christ's victory has an eternal effect on the righteous and the unrighteous alike. The effect on the righteous is positive. The effect on the unrighteous is also clear: "Then Death and Hades were cast into the lake of fire. This is the second death. And anyone not found written in the Book of life was cast into the lake of fire" (Rev. 20:14).

The good news is that believers will never see the place called hell, and they will never experience spiritual death. Hell and death are swallowed up and cast into the lake of fire. They have lost their sting. When the rapture takes place (the final catching up of Christians into heaven during the end-time) at the last trumpet, when Jesus comes back for his bride, the church, we will be changed as we meet him in the air. 1 Corinthians 15:51-55 brings clarity about this. "Behold I tell you a mystery: We shall not all sleep, but we (the righteous) shall all be changed—in a moment, in a twinkling of an eye, at the last trumpet. For the trumpet will sound, and the dead will be raised incorruptible, and we shall be changed. For this corruptible must put on incorruption, and this mortal has put on immortality. So when this corruptible has put on incorruption, and this mortal has put on immortality, then shall be brought to pass the saying that is written: 'Death is swallowed up in victory. O Death, where is your sting? O Hades, where is your victory?'"

Blasphemy

Why are Satan and his fallen angels consigned to such a stringent punishment as hell? Can they get a second chance—a chance to repent—such as we can? Is there no way they can be forgiven by God and given the opportunity to make things right? The answer to these questions is not good news for Satan and his followers. They have committed the unpardonable sin of blasphemy. They insulted God the Father by claiming they possessed the attributes of deity. They all saw God with their own eyes in all his glory, majesty, power, and splendor, and they still rebelled and rejected him. When the disciple Judas betrayed Jesus, he also committed blasphemy. He repented and afterwards hung himself. "Then Judas, His betrayer, seeing that He had been condemned, was remorseful and brought back the thirty pieces of silver to the chief priest and elders, saying, 'I have sinned by betraying innocent blood.' And they said, 'What is that to us? You see to it!'" (Matt. 27:3-4). Even though Judas repented, he could never be forgiven for betraying God to his face, just as Satan and his followers cannot be forgiven. His ending was filled with woes as Jesus said, "The Son of Man indeed goes just as it is written of Him, but woe to that man by whom the Son of Man is betrayed! It would have been better for that man (Judas) if he had not been born" (Matt. 26:24). The Bible is clear about the seriousness of this unforgivable sin. "Assuredly, I say to you, all sins will be forgiven the sons of men, and whatever blasphemies they may utter; but he who blasphemes against the Holy Spirit never has forgiveness, but is subject to eternal condemnation" (Mark 3:28-29). Judas is now suffering in hell and eventually he will be joined by Satan.

So why didn't God just kill Satan instead of allowing him to continue living? The answer is that God is using Satan, and all those who work for him, in the lives of his children to get glory and to teach us how to walk in dominion and authority in the earth again, like Adam was supposed to in the Garden. No one can be allowed to deny God to his face in heaven. Satan has been afforded a measure of time by God and he realizes he can never get another chance to disrupt the purposes of God in heaven. Therefore, he tries to disrupt the purposes of God on earth among human beings, God's image bearers. But the heavenly hour glass has been turned upside down for Satan, and he knows his time is drawing near. This is why he is working overtime to rob, kill, and destroy the people of God by any means necessary. In the meantime, the Devil and his army are working day and night to devour Christians. Satan, being the prince of the power of the air and a spirit, can travel faster than the speed of light. He and the sons of God (fallen angels) also have access to the throne of God, which they visit regularly to accuse the children of God (Job 1:6-12). Satan is a very dangerous foe of every believer, and though we do not have to fear him, we must respect his evil and destructive capabilities. "Be sober, be vigilant; because your adversary the devil walks about like a roaring lion, seeking whom he may devour. Resist him, steadfast in the faith, knowing that the same sufferings are experienced by your brotherhood in the world" (1 Pet. 5:8-9).

Some of Satan's angels are carrying out his orders over jurisdictions throughout the earth and in the lives of God's people. And some are chained up right now in Hades until Judgment Day to be cast into the fire along with Satan himself. "For if God did not spare the angels who sinned, but cast them down to Hell and delivered them into chains of darkness, to be reserved for judgment...*then* the Lord knows how to deliver the godly out of temptations and to reserve the unjust under punishment for the day of judgment, and especially those who walk according to the flesh in the lust of uncleanness and despise authority" (2 Pet. 2:4, 9-10).

Eligible for Damnation

Hell is a real place of torment and was originally designed for Satan and his fallen angels. They will, however, have more company on Judgment Day. According to the Bible, others who will join them include the wicked (Rom. 21:8), the disobedient (Rom. 2:8-9), the Beast and the False Prophet (Rev. 19:20), and worshipers of the Beast (Rev. 14:11).

How did human beings even become eligible for damnation? How did we get pulled into this equation? The answer is that hell is prepared for *all those* who reject Christ, as the gospel of Matthew makes clear when Jesus was speaking to his disciples: "And whoever will not receive you nor hear your words, when you depart from that house or city, shake off the dust from your feet. Assuredly, I say to you, it will be more tolerable for the land of Sodom and Gomorrah in the day of judgment than for that city!" (10:14-15).

This Scripture is very important because it shows there are different levels of punishment in hell. It also clears up some misconceptions about the types of people who will occupy hell. If hell is designed for *all* who reject Jesus Christ, this indicates that hell is not just for the so called "bad people." There will be some very "good people" there who have rejected the gospel of Christ as well. In fact, leaving room for everyone to be imperfect, there are some people who are not believers who live more moral and charitable lives than many Christians. Yet sadly, if they never make the decision to receive Christ as their personal Savior, their final eternal destination will be hell. This issue is one of the most controversial ones on the topic of the afterlife. The question most of us ask is, "Would a loving God send good people to hell"?

Most of us probably have no problem with God sending "bad" or "evil" people who reject Christ straight to hell. But "good" people? Even "good" people who reject Christ, just because they said "no thank you" to the gospel? Surely not the God of love, grace, and mercy. But as discussed earlier, God is a righteous and just God, and a God of balance. And hell is not chosen by God; we choose it freely.

Jesus is not Fire Insurance

As we have just mentioned, hell is not only for "bad people." One does not go to hell because of what one does, but because of what one believes. If a person does not believe Jesus is who he said he is, and that person dies apart from Jesus Christ as personal Lord and Savior, hell is the consequence. Therefore, the only sin that can send anyone to hell is the rejection of Jesus Christ. Hell was not designed by God for human beings in the first place, and good, bad, or ugly deeds do not send anyone to or keep anyone from hell. Who you have placed your faith in does. Believers, on the other hand, by God's grace have accepted Jesus and his teachings. Of course this gives no one a license to sin. We do not have permission to live any way we wish. Should the security of our salvation cause us to take advantage of the undeserved grace we have been given? Would it be worth breaking my fellowship with God even though my relationship with him is secure? The apostle Paul wrote "What shall we say then? Shall we continue in sin that grace may abound? Certainly not! How shall we who died to sin live any longer in it? Or do you know that as many of us as were baptized into Christ were baptized into His death? Therefore we were buried with him through baptism into death, that just as Christ was raised from the dead by the glory of the Father, even so we also should walk in the newness of life" (Rom. 6:11).

To think that we can continue to sin so God's grace will abound is treating Jesus Christ as if he were fire insurance. There are some Christians who think "It does not matter what I do that involves sin because God will forgive me." It is true that God will forgive us of any sin, but we must never forget there are painful consequences for our sins. God loves us, but he warns us in his Word of the devastation that sin can cause in our lives. If many of us had known ahead of time some of the consequences of our sinful decisions, we most likely would have made other choices. We are still dealing with the after effects of some of our bad choices after many, many years. This does not mean that God has not forgiven us if we have sincerely repented. Of course he has.

A lot of young people equate the forgiveness of God with escaping the consequences of sin. They think that if they did not escape the consequences of their sin then that means God does not love them and has not forgiven them. This is a tragic error. If I make a bad choice and run a red light, and then get caught by the police, the consequence of that offense is being given a traffic ticket. I can sincerely pray to God to forgive me for running the light, and he will. However, I will still be responsible for paying for that ticket because sin always has a debt that will be owed. Sin always has consequences. There is no sense getting angry with God for having to deal with the residue of our bad choices. It is the law of reaping and sowing; it is a life principle whether we are believers or nonbelievers. That is just the way it is. That is why we want to minimize our bad choices and try encouraging young people especially to make good choices. Nobody is perfect, but we cannot use imperfection as an excuse to continue making bad choices.

Sometimes we all make bad choices. But the one major bad choice we must never make is the one that affects eternity. Sincere, heartfelt repentances might allow us to escape the full impact of the consequences of our sin before we die. Yet still in the equation are repercussions that will have to be dealt with. In these few circumstances this just means that the situation did not turn out as bad as it could have. This is one of the reasons we get excited and praise God for his love, grace, and mercy that allows us to endure and survive things that normally would have done us in. Is this fair that some should escape the impact of their bad choices? Again, God is not fair when it comes to showering his blessings on us.

Progressive Sanctification

The mercy and grace of God's salvation compel us to want to live for God instead of living for the Devil. It is God's unconditional love that he has extended towards us when we did not deserve it that moves our hearts and minds to want to please him. What Christ did on the cross should not be viewed as something to be continually trampled on with an attitude of unrestrained liberty. God is longsuffering towards us due to his mercy and grace, but if we continue sinning without true repentance, we can be sure judgment will eventually follow. As Christians, we must learn to say no to some things. "For the grace of God that brings Salvation has appeared to all men, teaching us that, denying ungodliness and worldly lust, we should live soberly, righteously, and godly in the present age, looking for the blessed hope and glorious appearing of our great God and Savior Jesus Christ, Who gave Himself for us, that He might redeem us from every lawless deed and purify for

Himself His own special people, zealous for good works" (Titus 2:11-14).

All believers are undergoing a process of becoming purified. Throughout this progressive sanctification process we will not be sinless. Nor is God expecting us to be *sinless*, but he does expect us to continue to *sin less*. True biblical faith changes people. We cannot continue riding the "I'm not there yet" horse for the rest of our lives and giving ourselves the excuse to stay the way we are. We have to be very careful what sinful licenses we give ourselves because we will extend those same licenses to others around us and become a stumbling block to their spiritual growth and development. Ultimately, we have to remember that no matter what state a person is in, walking in the spirit or sinking deep in sin, they are never removed from God's love. Since God never removes anyone from his love, we certainly never can. We must extend grace to compel people to want to live right and to not become comfortable with continually living in sin.

God wants to first change what we are and then progressively change what we do. The most important thing is to allow him to change what we are by receiving him as personal Savior. What are we apart from Jesus Christ? We are sinners by nature (as descendants of Adam) whose sin has separated us from God. Therefore we need to place our faith and trust in the ultimate perfect sacrifice that not only redeemed us from our sin as children of disobedience, but satisfied the wrath and anger of God. Jesus paved the way in reconciling us back to God the Father by shedding his blood on the cross. "And according to the law almost all things are purified with blood, and without shedding of blood is no remission" (Heb. 9:22). "Therefore having been justified by faith, we have peace with God through our Lord Jesus Christ…Much more then, having now been justified by His blood, we shall be saved from wrath through Him. For if when we were enemies we were reconciled to God through the death of His Son, much more, having been reconciled, we shall be saved by His life. And not only that, but we also rejoice in God through our Lord Jesus Christ, through whom we have now received reconciliation" (Rom. 5:1, 9-11).

Jesus' Sacrifice

Jesus' sacrifice on the cross was so important to God the Father because he gave his only begotten Son to die in our deserved place. Hell was the deserved penalty for us all, but God in his mercy sent his Son in our place in order to give us a second chance at life. Hell is the penalty for choosing not to receive the free gift of salvation. This free gift is of no cost to us, but it cost Jesus his life. Logically, we have a hard time with anything we do not have to earn because we live in a world where you do not get something for nothing. Nothing is free and nothing comes easy—and if it does, there must be some catch to it. We are taught that we have to work for everything we get if we want to have it. But I beg to differ. When it comes to the free gift of salvation and eternal life in heaven, the only thing that is required is faith. Why? Because we cannot earn or buy something that is already paid for. The gift of salvation is not predicated on being a good person or bad person, because at the end of this life the only thing that will matter is one's eternal destiny based on faith and what he or she has done with the Son of God. If one has rejected Jesus, that choice will lead to hell, no matter if the person is good and full of integrity. This is not unfair because God is a God of balance who is fair enough to never leave anyone without a choice.

What this means is that a "bad" person could come to Christ before they die and still go to heaven. And a "good" person who does not come to Christ before they die can go to hell. We will all have to give an account to God for our lives, because, in the end, no one gets away with anything. Paul said so in Romans: "So then each of us shall give account of himself to God" (Rom. 14:12). God is the ultimate Judge of the living and the dead, for, as Peter said, "They will give an account to Him who is ready to judge the living and the dead" (1 Pet. 4:5).

We have said it is true that there are painful consequences for our sins. If someone commits murder and gets caught and convicted, the consequence is being sentenced to prison. If that murderer then comes to Christ, he or she will not be judged for their sin on Judgment Day. Why? Since their faith was placed in the finished work of Jesus Christ's death on the cross, the sin has been covered. For example, Moses was a credited believer when he committed murder. "Now it came to pass in those days, when Moses was grown, that he went out to his brethren and looked at their burdens. And he saw an Egyptian beating a Hebrew, one of his brethren. So he looked this way and that way, and when he saw no one, he killed the Egyptian and hid him in the sand" (Exod. 2:11-12). Later, Moses repented and accepted the call of God during a face to face encounter on Mt. Sinai. He was used to lead the Israelites out of slavery and into freedom. When Moses died, he went to heaven. He even made the hall of fame of faith in Hebrews 11. There is no spiritual double jeopardy—the saved person cannot be judged by God for his or her sins again because the sin was already paid for by Jesus' sacrifice on the cross. Then what will the murderer be judged for, and what sort of account will he or she have to give? The answer is found in Paul's second letter to the Corinthians: "Therefore we make it our aim, whether present or absent, to be well pleasing to Him. For we must all appear before the judgment seat of Christ, that each one may receive the things done in the body, according to what he has done, whether good or bad" (5:9-10). Paul's goal, to be well pleasing to God while living on earth, has Judgment Day seriousness attached to it.

This tells us that true faith leads to a changed life and that the believer's reward in connection to eternal security will be according to the things done in the body. "Now if anyone builds on this foundation with gold, silver, precious stones, wood, hay, straw, each one's work will become clear; for the Day will declare it, because it will be revealed by fire; and the fire will test each one's work, of what sort it is. If anyone's work which he has built on it endures, he will receive a reward. If anyone's work is burned, he will suffer loss; but he himself will be saved, yet so as through fire" (1 Cor. 3:12-15). Even though believers will not be sent to hell, there is still loss suffered on Judgment Day. For example, the loss of potential crowns received for works on earth that did not endure God's test of fire. "Now they do it to obtain a perishable crown, but we for an imperishable crown" (1 Cor. 9:25). The loss of crowns is detrimental because when we get to heaven the ones we receive for our good works will be cast at Jesus' feet as we glorify and worship him. There are various reasons that we can obtain crowns from God when we stand before him, but for our rewards that endure the test of fire, "Finally, there is laid up for me the crown of righteousness, which the Lord, the righteous Judge, will give to me on that Day, and not to me only but also to all who have loved His appearing" (2 Tim. 4:8). How we will be rewarded later depends on the life we live right now.

What Account Will We Give?

Fire insurance is better than no insurance at all, but the sense of urgency to live according to the Word of God should not diminish because "once we are saved we are always saved." This is not where our continuous motivation for Christian living should stop. What things done in the body will we have to give an account for? We will all be judged for every good or bad thought. "The LORD searches all hearts and understands all the intent of the thoughts. If you seek Him, He will be found by you; but if you forsake Him, He will cast you off forever" (1 Chron. 28:9). And we will be judged for every good or idol word spoken: "But I say to you that for every idle word men may speak, they will give account of it in the day of judgment" (Matt. 12:36). We will also be judged for every good or bad motive: "For the LORD does not see as man sees; for man looks at the outward appearance, but the LORD looks at the heart" (1 Sam. 16:7). Last but not least, as mentioned earlier, we will all be judged for every good or bad deed: "The fire will test each one's work, of what sort it is. If anyone's work which he has built on it endures, he will receive a reward. If anyone's work is burned, he will suffer loss; but he himself will be saved, yet so as through fire" (1 Cor. 3:13-15).

We will also have to give an account to God for what kind of stewards we were in life, and what we did with the things entrusted to us. We will be disciplined according to the depth of our knowledge of God's will, and our obedience to that will. The more we have been given, the more will be required: "And that servant who knew his master's will, and did not prepare *himself* or do according to his will, shall be beaten with many *stripes*. But he who did not know, yet committed things deserving of stripes, shall be beaten with few. For everyone to whom much is given, from him much will be required; and to whom much has been committed, of him they will ask the more" (Luke 12:47-48).

Ultimately, we will receive our deserved rewards in accordance with God's evaluation of our lives, which is something also confirmed by Scripture. "Then I saw a great white throne and Him who sat on it, from whose face the earth and the heavens fled away. And there was found no place for them. And I saw the dead, small and great, standing before God, and books were opened. And another book was opened, which is the Book of life. And the dead were judged according to their works, by the things that were written in the books" (Rev. 20:11-12). Everyone will stand before God after they die to give an account of their lives before being sentenced. "It is appointed unto man to die once, but after this the judgment" (Heb. 9:27). "For we shall all stand before the judgment seat of Christ" (2 Cor. 5:10). The question is, will we be standing before God as unrighteous persons giving an account for our sin, only to be sent to hell, or as righteous persons, who will account for our works and spend eternity in heaven?

Eternal Security

It is true we will be judged for everything we think and do. But despite what we think or do, no one and nothing can snatch us out of God's hand. This is confirmed in John 10:28-30: "And I give them eternal life, and they shall never perish: neither shall anyone snatch them out of My hand. My Father, who has given them to Me, is greater than all; and no one is able to snatch them out of my Father's hand. I and My father are one." Not even one who commits suicide without the chance to ask God for forgiveness can snatch themselves out of the Father's hands. In fact, when most people die they do not get the chance to ask for forgiveness for every sin they have ever committed every day of their lives. God does not supersede our free will to choose whether we are believers or nonbelievers, and he is not an Indian giver who would give us salvation and then change his mind because of something we did. Christ's death on the cross is sufficient to cover all the sin of the world, and that is what makes salvation, grace, and mercy what they are—undeserved favor God chooses to shower on us.

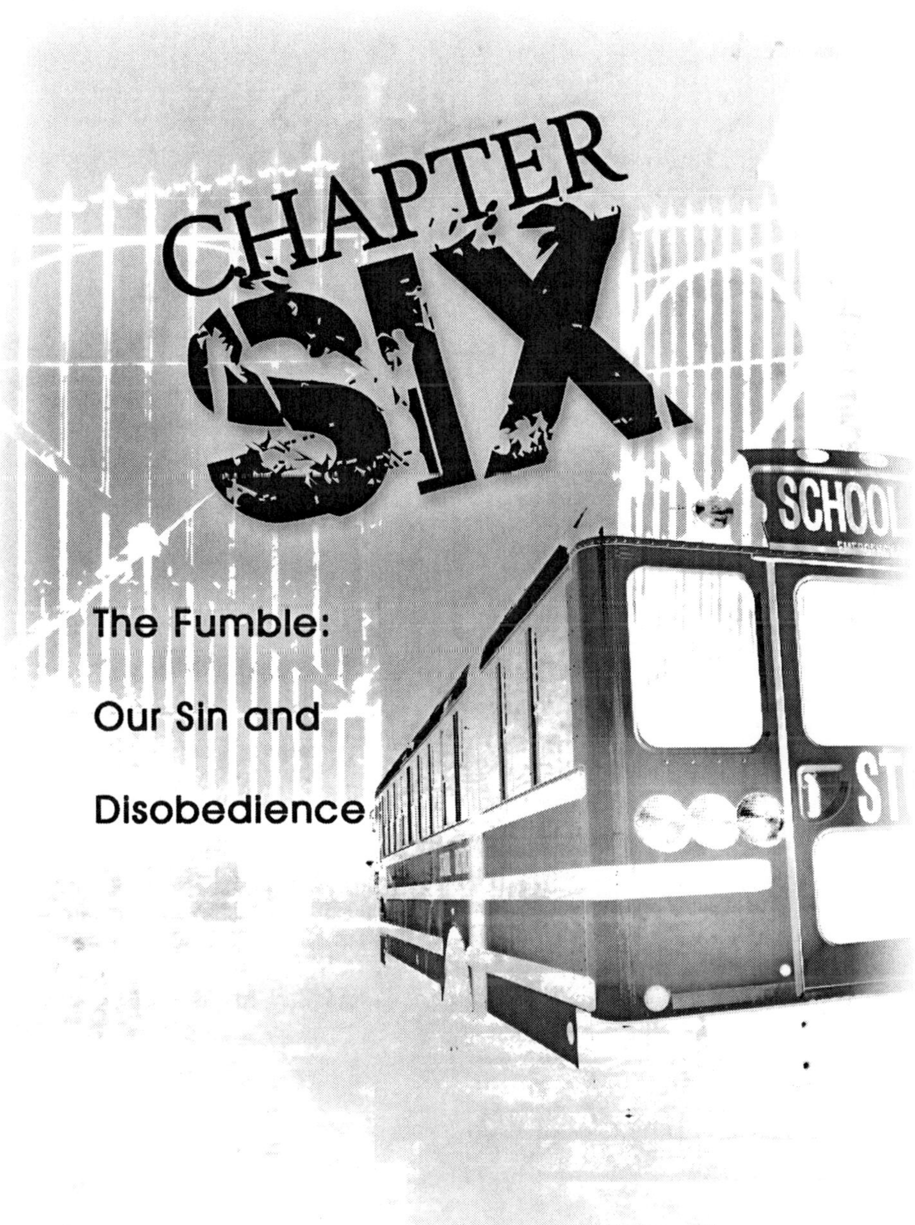

CHAPTER SIX

The Fumble: Our Sin and Disobedience

If God's original design for hell was for Satan and his fallen angels, as we have already discussed, then how did humans become possible participants in this place of torment, suffering, and pain? Let us go back to Genesis, the beginning of the Bible. Eve was deceived by the serpent into taking the fruit from the forbidden tree in the garden. Adam did the same thing, except that because God gave him the instructions and responsibility personally, he sinned willfully and without deception. This is confirmed in the first letter of Paul to Timothy: "For Adam was formed first, then Eve. And Adam was not deceived, but the woman being deceived, fell into transgression" (1 Tim. 2:13-14). Prior to this happening, God established his first covenant with Adam. This covenant is recorded in the book of Genesis: "Then God blessed them, and God said to them, 'Be fruitful and multiply; fill the earth and subdue it; have dominion over the fish of the sea, over the birds of the air, and over every living thing that moves on the earth.' And God said, 'See, I have given you every herb that yields seed which is on the face of all the earth, and every tree whose fruit yields seed; to you it shall be for food. Also, to every beast of the earth, to every bird of the air, and to everything that creeps on the earth, in which there is life, I have given every green herb for food'; and it was so" (1:28-30). "And the LORD God commanded the man, saying, 'Of every tree of the garden you may freely eat; but of the tree of the knowledge of good and evil you shall not eat, for in the day that you eat of it you shall surely die'" (Gen. 2:16-17).

The conditions of the covenant are clear. One, Adam and Eve were to populate the earth by being fruitful and multiplying; two, they were to subdue the earth; three, they were to have dominion over the created animals; four, they were to tend and care for the Garden and enjoy its fruit; and, five, they were not to eat the fruit from the tree of the knowledge of good and evil, or else they would die. But this covenant ended when the original human pair ate the fruit of the tree of knowledge of good and evil. Because of their disobedience and rebellion, and more specifically the disobedience and rebellion of Adam, the end result was humankind's inevitable spiritual and physical deaths. Therefore, God had to establish another covenant with the human race.

This means it was Adam who fumbled the ball and cost the game for all humankind. In his letter to the Romans, Paul wrote, "Therefore, just as through one man sin entered the world, and death through sin, and thus death spread to all men, because all sinned—for until the law sin was in the world, but sin is not imputed when there is no law. Nevertheless death reigned from Adam to Moses, even over those who had not sinned according to the likeness of the transgression of Adam, who is a type of Him who was to come" (5:12-14).

As a result of this failure, God made another covenant, or compact, with Adam. This covenant can also be called *the covenant with humankind* because it sets forth the conditions that will be held until the curse of sin is lifted by the coming Messiah, Jesus Christ. The covenant is recorded in Genesis 3:14-21: "So the LORD God said to the serpent: 'Because you have done this, you are cursed more than all cattle, and more than every beast of the field; on your belly you shall go, and you shall eat dust all the days of your life. And I will put enmity between you and the woman, and between your seed and her Seed; He shall bruise your head, and you shall bruise His heel.' To the woman He said: 'I will greatly multiply your sorrow and your conception; in pain you shall bring forth children; your desire shall be for your husband, and he shall rule over you.' Then to Adam He said, 'Because you have heeded the voice of your wife, and have eaten from the tree of which I commanded you, saying, 'You shall not eat of it': Cursed is the ground for your sake; in toil you shall eat of it all the days of your life. Both thorns and thistles it shall bring forth for you, and you shall eat the herb of the field. In the sweat of your face you shall eat bread till you return to the ground, for out of it you were taken; for dust you are, and to dust you shall return.' And Adam called his wife's name Eve, because she was the mother of all living. Also for Adam and his wife the LORD God made tunics of skin, and clothed them."

The conditions of this covenant are also clear. One, the serpent is cursed and the indwelling energizer of the serpent is cursed as well. Two, the first prophecy of the coming Messiah is given. Three, there would be multiple conceptions by women, which would introduce death into the human race. Four, there would now be pain in childbirth. Five, the woman's relationship with her husband is now flawed. Six, the ground is cursed and brings forth weeds among the food people must eat for their existence. Seven, the creation resists man's efforts to maintain it, and he must toil in frustration for the rest of his life. Eight, because of sin there is now both physical and spiritual death. As the flesh decays, men and women return to the dust from which God created them.

And yet, with all the covenant entails, God still extends his grace and mercy, even though Adam and Eve are driven out of the Garden of Eden and prevented from ever returning. It may seem counterintuitive, but this was done for their protection. Now that they knew good and evil as a result of eating from the forbidden tree, removing them from the garden removed them from the temptation of eating from the tree again and being locked into a sinful state forever. If this had happened, all humankind would have been destined for destruction in hell, with no hope for a second chance. We find this out in Genesis 3:22-24: "Then the Lord God said, 'Behold, the man has become like one of Us, to know good and evil. And now, lest he put out his hand and take also of the tree of life, and eat, and live forever'—therefore the Lord God sent him out of the garden of Eden to till the ground from whence he was taken. So He drove out the man; and He placed cherubim at the east of the garden of Eden, and a flaming sword which turned every way, to guard the way to the tree of life."

Fumbling the Ball

Because of sin and disobedience, humankind was separated from God and now has a severed fellowship with him.

Everyone who would come after Adam as his descendants would inherit a sin nature, making us sinners who need to be saved from ourselves. Even little babies have a sin nature. The psalmist writes, "Behold, I was brought forth in iniquity, and in sin my mother conceived me" (Ps. 51:5). I easily accepted this theology after having babysat my little niece Brianna a few times while she was going through her "terrible twos" stage. However, the Bible does not support infants, babies, and small children being sent to hell because of their sin natures. Matthew 18:14 says, "Even so it is not the will of your Father who is in heaven that one of these little ones should perish." And Jesus said, "Let the little children come to Me, and do not forbid them; for of such is the kingdom of God" (Mark 10:14).

God is just and fair, and he would never send infants, babies, and small children to hell because of their lack of cognitive development. Children, being underdeveloped not only cognitively but intellectually, emotionally, and in their will, are not capable of understanding spiritual matters. In the book of Hosea it says, "My people are destroyed for lack of knowledge. Because you have rejected knowledge, I also will reject you from being priest for Me" (4:6) This Scripture is referring to those who already have a mature level of understanding and make a decision to reject God anyway. In order to reject something, there is an evaluation process that goes on in the mind that makes one conclude they do not want what they are rejecting. With this said, there is an understanding of what is being rejected. Infants, babies, and little children do not have the capacity to understand spiritual principles, and this is true even if they accept or reject Christ. Therefore, they have a qualified exemption to heaven in the event that they die.

Imagine Adam fumbling the ball at the beginning of human history. In football there is one bad play deemed to be in a category all alone. This bad play represents the ultimate dejection, embarrassment, and humiliation for any football player. That play is the fumble—dropping the ball or failing to handle it correctly. It is especially egregious when, after a fumble, the other team recovers the ball, and it is a doubly flagrant error if they recover the fumble and run it back for a touchdown. In this football analogy, God handed Adam the ball when he gave him instructions pertaining to the two trees in the Garden of Eden. But Adam failed to handle the ball properly by disobeying God's instructions, costing Adam and Eve and their descendants the game of life. This fumble also made us candidates for a place of torments called hell. Keeping in mind this football analogy, let us take a look at the Scriptures to see just how sin entered the world and brought about the fall of man. Imagine with me the "Super Bowl in the Beginning."

The Fall of Man

Genesis 1:1 says, "In the beginning God created the heavens and the earth." The Bible makes it clear from the very beginning that the sovereign God is the author of existence and in charge of everything. He establishes himself as CEO, owner, general manager, coach, defensive coordinator, and offensive coordinator. In the game of life, he plays every position on the field, including quarterback.

As the quarterback, he calls the plays in the huddle on the field of life.

There was a need for lights so the game could be played. Thus, "Then God said, 'Let there be light'; and there was light. And God saw the light, that it was good; and God divided the light from the darkness. God called the light Day, and the darkness He called Night. So the evening and the morning were the first day" (Gen. 1:3-5).

Then God as the general manager created some players for the human team. "God said, 'Let Us make man in Our image, according to Our likeness; let them have dominion over the fish of the sea, over the birds of the air, and over the cattle, and over all the earth, and over every creeping thing that creeps on the earth.' So God created man in His own image; in the image of God created He him; male and female He created them" (Gen. 1:26-27). Man and woman became the Father's draft picks who would play for the Godhead.

A premier player was needed for the team, an All-Creation running back who could carry the ball into action. Adam was that player. "And the Lord God formed man of the dust of the ground, and breathed into his nostrils the breath of life; and man became a living being" (Gen. 2:7). Adam was the Creator's number one draft pick who, after God breathed into him the breath of life, would carry the ball in the garden and the game of life.

God created the gridiron (the field) that the game of life would be played on. "The Lord planted a garden eastward in Eden..." (Gen. 2:8a).

Next God put the team, along with Adam, on the field, "...and there He put the man whom he had formed" (Gen. 2:8b).

Now the game is ready to begin. Team God wins the coin toss and opts to receive the ball.

God the Father as quarterback calls a play in the huddle as he looks at Adam and says, "Adam, we are giving you the ball and we are going to run your play." "And the Lord God commanded the man, saying, 'Of every tree of the garden you may freely eat; but of the tree of the knowledge of good and evil you shall not eat, for in the day that you eat of it you shall surely die'" (Gen. 2:16-17). "You got that?" Adam shook his head yes and the team said in unison, "Break," as they gave one clap of their hands and proceeded to line up in formation on the line of scrimmage. God the Father as quarterback said, "Willing Obedience 42, Willing Obedience 42, ready, set, hike-hike. He dropped back two steps into the pocket, faked a pass to creation, and handed the ball off to Adam—who began carrying out his running instructions.

Having foresight, God knew that if Adam was going to successfully carry the ball he would need some help. He would need someone assisting him on every play by blocking as he carried the ball for Team God. That is why "The Lord God said, 'It is not good for man to be alone; I will make him a helper comparable to him'" (Gen. 2:18).

In order to create this helper, "The Lord God caused a deep sleep to fall upon Adam, and he slept; and He took one of his ribs, and closed up the flesh in its place. Then the rib, which the Lord God had taken from man He made into a woman, and He brought her to the man" (Gen. 2:21-22). In this way God created Adam's helper and lead blocker, Eve.

Where there is offense, there is defense. A deceptive defensive blitz was called by the Enemy to neutralize the play God had called on the field. The defense started trash-talking while blitzing when Satan approached Eve while the play was in motion. He questioned the play God called. "And he said to the woman, Has God indeed said, 'You shall not eat of every tree of the garden?'" Eve is deceived at this point, and she misconstrues the truth. "Then the serpent said to the woman, 'You will not surely die. For God knows that in the day you eat of it your eyes will be opened, and you will be like Gods, knowing good and evil'" (Gen. 3:1, 4-5).

Eve, the lead blocker for Team God, lined up out of position and offside, and she is called for a penalty. "So when the woman saw that the tree was good for food, that it was pleasant to the eyes, and a tree desirable to make one wise, she took of its fruit and ate" (Gen. 3:6a). Then God the Father, as referee, threw the yellow penalty flag as the play continued to develop.

As Adam carried the ball, Eve took the fruit from the tree, ate, and then she offered it to Adam. "She also gave to her husband with her, and he ate" (Gen. 3:6b). Adam got hit hard and coughed up the ball, and both teams on the field yelled FUMBLE! There was a scramble for the loose ball, and Satan and his deceptive defensive blitz recovered it. This brought Adam and humankind the ultimate defeat, as Satan and his team had possession of the football—with the lead and with no time left on the clock. The human race had lost, and this was all due specifically to Adam's willful sin and disobedience to God. Whereas humankind was in a state of spiritual and physical perfection, now it had become sin-sick, sin-cursed, and fallen. The ultimate consequence was hell for Adam, Eve, and all of their descendants—unless, that is, a perfect sacrifice could be made to appease God's wrath.

When all hope seemed lost, unexpectedly and just in time, Jesus, the substitute coach, came out of nowhere and took center stage on the field. Now on the sideline with all eyes watching, Jesus pulled out the red flag stained with his shed blood on the cross and threw it down on the ground to challenge the play on the field. God the Father, as referee, sees the red flag. He stops, looks, turns up his microphone and announces, "Team God is challenging the play on the field." God the referee went to talk it over with the other three referees, goodness, grace, and mercy, and then he proceeded to the instant replay booth to re-examine the play on the field. It took God the Father three days to examine the play and decide on the final outcome of the game because of Jesus' death, burial, and his early Sunday morning resurrection. After the review, he announced into the microphone, "After further review, 'For God so loved the world that He gave His only begotten Son, that whoever believes in Him should not perish but have everlasting life' (John 3:16). Put more time on the clock, Team God will be awarded a first down." Then he signaled with his arm in the direction of Team God. Thus human beings got an undeserved second chance and another opportunity to win the game.

A Second Chance

There was a testimony given by a famous visiting preacher in my former church one Wednesday during a revival. He told the story of a young man who played football in high school. It was the state championship game and the team that had the ball was down and needed a touchdown to win. The time was quickly winding down. So they called a play for their star running back, who eventually fumbled the ball. Luckily, the star player who fumbled the ball recovered it. The coach called time-out and each team headed towards the sideline to get some water and rest for what would appear to be the last play of the game. The player who had just fumbled the ball hung his head low and was bothered by the fact that he had almost lost the game for his team. The coach, seeing this and still believing in his star player, came over to him and said, "Keep your head up, son. We are going to run that same play again, but to the opposite side this time." The player's face lit up like the sun as he and the rest of his teammates put their helmets on and ran back on the field to set up the play. Many in the crowd noticed they were lined up in the same formation as the previous play that almost caused a turn over, and they realized the team was running the same play as before. Even the home team crowd began booing as they expected the same negative outcome. At the snap of the ball, the quarterback handed off to the star running back, who ran in for a touchdown with almost no time remaining on the clock. His team kicked a field goal, which won and sealed the game, making them the state champions.

After the celebration eventually calmed down, the reporters made their way to the locker room to interview the running back whose team won the state championship. The reporters had the same question. They asked, "What made you run like that? We've never seen you run like that before." With tears in his eyes, the player said, "He gave me a second chance."

A New Covenant

Despite the disobedience and failure that brought sin into the world, we have all been given a second chance to become winners at the game of life. God loves us unconditionally and he extends love, grace, and mercy to us all by way of Jesus Christ and his atoning death on the cross. His shed blood has justified us, redeemed us, saved us, and reconciled us back to God. He has entered into a new covenant with us, and he has forgiven our sin and remembers it no more: "Behold, the days are coming, says the LORD, when I will make a new covenant with the house of Israel and with the house of Judah—...But this is the covenant that I will make with the house of Israel after those days, says the LORD: I will put My law in their minds, and write it on their hearts; and I will be their God, and they shall be My people. No more shall every man teach his neighbor, and every man his brother, saying, 'Know the LORD,' for they all shall know Me, from the least of them to the greatest of them, says the LORD. For I will forgive their iniquity, and their sin I will remember no more" (Jer. 31:31, 33-34).

But sin has its consequences. Even with a second chance, sometimes life can be complicated with spiritual, mental, emotional, physical, marital, and financial suffering and pain. However, despite the troubles and tribulations we may face in this present life, those of us who have turned to Christ and put our trust in the finished work he did on the cross can testify that not only do we have help and comfort down here on earth, but we will never have to worry about experiencing hell in the next life. Faith in Jesus Christ means we are no longer potential participants in that place.

CHAPTER SEVEN

Straight from the Church: Without Any Excuse

People can go to hell straight from the church. That may sound odd, but it is true. All those who profess to be Christians and who are active in the church should search their hearts to make sure they actually are believers. One cannot take for granted that everyone in church is saved, even those in leadership positions. God is the ultimate judge on who is and who is not a true member of the body of Christ, and he is the ultimate authority on everyone's eternal destination. But knowing for sure is not a bad thing.

It is possible that people we assume are Christians are not and, conversely, people we think are not believers truly are. This chapter focuses on those who may be active in the church but who are really not believers in Jesus Christ. It is sad to say, but if their salvation status does not change while there is still a chance for it to change, they will wind up being damned through the church. We will consider those who come to church on either a regular or non-regular basis, who hear sermon after sermon, and always decide not to respond to the inner impulse of the Holy Spirit. And we will consider those who are church members—maybe even church leaders—who are not Christians, either. This could include church volunteers, congregational leaders, deacons, elders, trustees, associate ministers, and even some pastors and bishops.

It should not surprise us that there are many people who work in the church who are actually unbelievers. Satan's deception does not stop at the doors of the organized church. What a tragedy it would be to live a life thought to be in line with Christ, only to find out that Christ never knew the person. What a tragedy it would be for one to have lived a life where many things were done for God and in his name, only to find out the good done was not in his name at all. And what a tragedy it would be to stand alone before God to give an account of one's life only to discover one's name is not written in the Lamb's Book of Life. When God pulls up our resume of works, and as we try negotiating with him and pleading our way into heaven, our sentence will be instead to hell. This scenario does not have to represent any of us, but it could. The choice is ours.

The Wheat and the Tares

The saddest reality in life is the fact that people are dying and going to hell. An even sadder reality is the fact that some we perceive as Christians are also going to hell—straight from the church. I am not talking about what is called the "church universal," or all true Christian believers around the world. The church universal is the body of Christ. The phrase "straight from the church" as it is used here refers to the local, organized, or institutional church—the place or building where many opportunities traditionally present themselves each week to hear the gospel message and to take advantage of the chance to come to faith. That is why those who continually forfeit these chances, for whatever reason, are utterly without any excuse. They will never be able to stand before God and say in truth, "I did not know," or "I never had the chance."

Of course, the local church is not the only place one can become a Christian. That can be done anywhere at any time. All that is required is a prayer of confession and repentance sincerely from the heart to God, asking him for salvation. But our focus will be those inside the local church where the body of Christ gathers. It is time the church examined itself to see who accepts the gospel and who does not. God's Word tells us that "The time has come for judgment to begin at the house of God; and if it begins with us first, what will be the end of those who do not obey the Gospel of God? Now 'If the righteous one is scarcely saved, Where will the ungodly and the sinner appear?' Therefore let those who suffer according to the will of God commit their souls to Him in doing good, as to a faithful Creator" (1 Pet. 4:17-19).

The term *church* in its proper context refers to the church universal, or the body of Christ. We must keep in mind that the body of Christ is not specifically a building. Rather, it refers to believers the world over. They are the "called out ones" (that is what "church" means in the Greek). Here we are not talking about the "called out ones." We are talking about those who come to church buildings all across the land who are not part of the body of Christ. They are around the building where the body of Christ congregates, and they may be an integral part of how the local church functions. But they are not believers. The way the Bible puts it, they are not "saved." Some will end up dying in the state of unbelief and going to hell. This is not a judgmental statement, and it can be supported from three arguments: Satan's duplication power, Satan's deception power, and Satan's deferring power, all of which assist in people going to hell straight from the church.

Satan's Duplication Power

According to the Word of God, the righteous and the wicked will co-exist and grow together in the local church. The gospel of Matthew confirms this in the parable of the wheat and the tares: "Another Parable He put forth to them, saying: 'The kingdom of heaven is like a man who sowed seeds in his field; but while men slept, his enemy came and sowed tares among the wheat and went his way. But when the grain had sprouted and produced crop, then the tares also appeared. So the servants of the owner came and said to him, 'Sir, did you not sow good seed in your field? How then does it have tares?' He said to them, 'An enemy has done this.' The servants said to him, 'Do you want us then to go and gather them up?' But he said, 'No, lest while you gather up the tares you also uproot the wheat with them. Let both grow together until the harvest, and at the time of harvest I will say to the reapers, 'First gather the tares and bind them in bundles to burn them, but gather the wheat into my barn'" (13:24-30).

That the wheat (the righteous) and the tares (the wicked) exist side-by-side in the local church shows Satan's duplication power. Both will continue growing together so the righteous will not get uprooted when trying to gather up the wicked. This will occur until God calls for his reapers to separate and gather them for the harvest judgment. The wicked will be gathered together to be burned in hell, and the righteous will be gathered together in heaven. Here is how the apostle John saw things: "Then I looked, and behold, a white cloud, and on the cloud sat One like the Son of Man, having on His head a golden crown, and in His hand a sharp sickle. And another angel came out of the temple, crying with a loud voice to Him who sat on the cloud, 'Thrust in Your sickle and reap, for the time has come for You to reap, for the harvest of the earth is ripe." So He who sat on the cloud thrust in His sickle on the earth, and the earth was reaped. Then another angel came out of the temple which is in heaven, he also having a sharp sickle. And another angel came out from the altar, who had power over fire, and he cried with a loud cry to him who had the sharp sickle, saying, 'Thrust in your sharp sickle and gather the clusters of the vine of the earth, for her grapes are fully ripe.' So the angel thrust his sickle into the earth and gathered the vine of the earth, and threw it into the great winepress of the wrath of God. And the winepress was trampled outside the city, and blood came out of the winepress, up to the horses' bridles, for one thousand six hundred furlongs" (Rev. 14:14-20).

Satan is an impersonator and has been so from the beginning of time. It was his prideful desire to want to impersonate God, or be like the Most High, that got him and his followers kicked out of heaven in the first place. Satan said, "I will ascend above the heights of the clouds, I will be like the Most High" (Isa. 14:14). Even in his fallen state, Satan is able to impersonate. That was certainly true when he took the character and form of the serpent when he deceived Eve into partaking of the forbidden fruit. Before this, the serpent used to walk upright, but now it crawls on its belly because it has been humbled and defeated. "The LORD God said to the serpent: 'Because you have done this, You are cursed more than all cattle, And more than every beast of the field; On your belly you shall go, And you shall eat dust All the days of your life" (Gen. 3:14). At one time the serpent was a desirable creature; now it is considered hideous.

Thus Satan is no stranger to impersonation and duplication, and he is still in the business of doing these things even to this day. The second epistle of Timothy says, "But evil men and imposters will grow worse and worse, deceiving and being deceived (3:13). The Bible also tells us that Satan is full of beauty and wisdom and can even transform himself into an angel of light. In other words, he is able to conjure up that which looks like God, sounds like God, and appears to be God, and he can wreck and ruin lives in the process. He is the apex of the false apostle. Paul said, "For such are false apostles, deceitful workers, transforming themselves into apostles of Christ. And no wonder! For Satan himself is transformed into an angel of light. Therefore it is no great thing if his ministers also be transformed as the ministers of righteousness, whose end will be according to their works" (2 Cor. 11:13-15).

Satan's people are energized by him to do his bidding inside and outside the local church, and we must always be on the lookout. We read in the gospel of Matthew to "Beware of false prophets, who come to you in sheep's clothing, but inwardly they are ravenous wolves. You will know them by their fruits. Do men gather grapes from thorn bushes, or figs from thistles? Even so, every good tree bears good fruit, but a bad tree bears bad fruit. A good tree cannot bear bad fruit, nor can a bad tree bear good fruit. Every tree that does not bear good fruit is cut down, and thrown into the fire. Therefore by their fruits you will know them" (Matt. 7:15-20).

We cannot judge anyone's hearts or motives, for only God can do that. But we are told to judge a person's fruit or behavior. This helps us to identify false teachers and be separate from them. Paul wrote "not to keep company with anyone named a brother, who is sexually immoral, or covetous, or an idolater, or a reviler, or a drunkard, or an extortioner—not even to eat with such a person. For what have I to do with judging those also who are outside? Do you not judge those who are inside? But those who are outside God judges. Therefore 'put away from yourselves the evil person'" (1 Cor. 5:11-13). This is called righteous judgment, and it is explained in Matthew 7:24 where the Bible tells us, "Do not judge according to appearance, but judge with righteous judgment." Further, it says, "Hypocrite! First remove the plank from your own eye, and then you will see clearly to remove the speck from your brother's eye" (Matt. 7:5). This allows us to discern the pretenders from the proven.

The more we allow the Word of God to expose us to ourselves first, and allow God, through the power of the Holy Spirit, to remove our sins, the more we put ourselves in a position to make righteous judgments in someone else's life. The more we are open, honest, and transparent with God about ourselves, then and only then are we able to know, see, and judge a brother's or sister's behavioral fruit. We are not to condemn anyone or make them feel low but instead extend a balance of love and accountability to them as we make our assessment. If only love is extended, this would not express an urgency to change. On the other hand, if only accountability is extended, this would be perceived as overwhelming condemnation. Interestingly enough, if handled like this, in both cases there is a risk of losing that person instead of gaining them. In fact, the ultimate goal of righteous judging is to get the person back on track, as Paul says. "Brethren, if a man is overtaken in any trespass, you who are spiritual restore such a one in a spirit of gentleness, considering yourself lest you also be tempted" (Gal. 6:1). This caution helps to never make anyone feel as if they have no value, even when they walk in error.

The truth is that we cannot afford *not* to judge righteously. Satan's duplication power makes this mandatory. He has his own workers in the local church, and the spiritual health and well being of the true body of Christ is at stake. "Do not be deceived: 'Evil company corrupts good habits'" (Cor. 15:33). We also need to judge righteously because we live out what we believe, and if we believe untruth, we live that out as well. However, only the truth of God's Word can make us free indeed. Satan's workers would not want us to learn the truth of God's Word, which sets the stage for our next point.

Satan's Deception Power

There are people who sit under the teaching of the Word on a regular basis who still choose not to respond to the prompting of the Holy Spirit. Perhaps they think they have valid reasons in their own minds. What allows them to try getting along without the help of God? It is Satan's deception power operating in their lives and influencing their blinded minds. In Paul's second letter to the Corinthians, he writes about those "whose minds the god of this age has blinded, who do not believe, lest the light of the gospel of the glory of Christ, who is the image of God, should shine on them" (4:4). Satan is able to keep people spiritually blinded, thus preventing them from getting saved. "He has blinded their eye, and hardened their hearts, lest they should see with their eyes, lest they should understand with their hearts and turn, so that I should heal them" (John 12:40). Satan uses many different tricks to keep people in a blinded state.

What reasons do people give for not responding to the gospel? Here are forty of them:

1. *I've been going to church all my life.*
2. *I was baptized when I was little.*
3. *I grew up in the church.*
4. *I give money to the church faithfully.*
5. *God knows my heart.*
6. *My mom and dad are saved.*
7. *My parents are church leaders.*

8. *I'm a church leader.*
9. *I work for the church.*
10. *I have been serving in ministry for a long time.*
11. *I was dedicated to the Lord when I was little.*
12. *I went to Sunday school every week when I was little.*
13. *I went to Vacation Bible School every summer.*
14. *I sang in the choir.*
15. *I've been preaching for many years.*
16. *I'm afraid.*
17. *I'm embarrassed.*
18. *Everybody already thinks that I'm saved.*
19. *I'm too messed up—God can't save me.*
20. *I know if I get saved, I'll still be out there sinning again, so I'd rather not.*
21. *I'll get saved when I'm older.*
22. *I'm too young for that stuff.*
23. *I'm not ready yet.*
24. *The church is a bunch of hypocrites.*
25. *The church takes up too many offerings.*
26. *The Pastor is probably stealing money.*
27. *The Pastor drives an expensive car.*
28. *I know about sin among church leadership from a previous church.*

29. *I know too many bad examples from previous churches I've attended.*
30. *I don't understand the Word or the Sermon.*
31. *I'm the Pastor's child—what will people think?*
32. *I live a morally good life.*
33. *I try to help everybody.*
34. *I treat people well—I'm a good person.*
35. *Church is too long.*
36. *I do more good deeds than I do bad deeds.*
37. *I have too much sin in my life.*
38. *People will look down on me and judge me.*
39. *I had a bad church experience before.*
40. *People will talk about me.*

Of course this list can go on, and all these reasons (and many others) are real and understandable. Still, when this life is over we will all have to stand by ourselves before God and give an account about what we have done with his Son Jesus. And on that day, God himself might also agree that some of these reasons are legitimate ones for failing to come to Christ. Nevertheless, all God will be concerned about at that moment is what we have done in relation to believing in his Son, Jesus Christ. What reasons would we list to justify remaining in unbelief? If there are any, we need to make sure we are true members of the body of Christ. It is better to be saved than to be sorry.

Satan's Deferring Power

The issue of going to hell straight from the church is very serious. Satan's deferring power will show us just how serious it is. We already know the enemy wants to distort the Word like he did with Eve in the garden. Satan gave Eve some truth, embedded in some lies, which made the entire statement a lie. While communicating with Satan, Eve misconstrued the truth that God gave to Adam. God never told Adam and Eve not to touch the tree of knowledge of good and evil or they would surely die. He told them not to eat of it, because on the day they ate of it they would surely die (Gen. 3:3).

What exactly does Satan want to defer? He wants to defer the truth of God's Word from getting down in our hearts and taking root. He wants this because he knows that knowing the truth of God's Word makes us free (John 8:32). The truth of God's Word will awaken our blinded minds to receive the Holy Spirit's enlightenment and realize that we need to be saved. Knowing the truth of God's Word will also give us a fresh perspective. It will soften our hard hearts to receive Christ as our personal Savior, ultimately freeing us from hell, *the penalty of sin.* Another thing Satan wants to defer is our growth in grace. As we grow spiritually, God will gradually free us from *the power of sin* in our lives. Because of salvation, sin does not have ultimate power over us anymore, even though we fall short at times. When we get to heaven we will spend eternity with him and be free from *the presence of sin.* This, too, Satan wishes to defer. He knows the Scripture in John 8:31-32 and 36 which says, "Then Jesus said to those Jews who believed Him, 'If you abide in My word, you are my disciples indeed. And you shall know the truth, and the truth shall make you free.' ...Therefore if the Son makes you free, you shall be free indeed." All this Satan wants to defer.

The enemy wants to defer the Word of God from getting down in our hearts and taking root so that he can continue keeping us blinded and bound. If we continue to stay blinded and bound, we will not be made free to receive God's enlightenment to understand that we need to be saved. Satan, knowing that his days are numbered, wants to blind and bind as many people as he can so they will not be rescued.

The parable of the sower and the seed in Matthew 13 gives us some concrete evidence as to how Satan is able to defer the Word of God from taking root in the hearts of people who attend church regularly. The parable deals with a sower who went out and regularly sowed seeds on four types of soils. The sower represents all those who share the seed, and the seed represents the Word of God. The four types of soil are the four types of hearts that the seed falls on regularly. When we think in terms of regularly sowing or hearing the Word, we generally think of worship in the local church. But people can listen to God's Word in many different places, such as on the radio, television, computers, or even on portable electronics. Still, for our purposes, we will assume that the process of sowing and hearing regularly takes place most often in a local church setting. People hear the seed of the Word as it falls on four types of soils (or hearts) and produces a result. The first soil or heart is *the wayside*, which is described in Matthew's gospel:

"And as he sowed, some seed fell by the wayside; and the birds of the air came and devoured them…When anyone hears the word of the kingdom, and does not understand it, then the wicked one comes and snatches away what was sown in his heart. This is he who received seed by the wayside" (13:4, 19).

We learn from this passage of Scripture that Satan uses ignorance and lack of understanding to defer the Word of God from the hearts of those who hear it, preventing them from taking root spiritually. The person who receives the seed by the wayside remains apart from Christ and his church, and can end up going to hell straight from the church.

The second soil or heart is *the stony place*, as described in the same chapter of Matthew: "Some fell on stony places, where they did not have much earth: and they immediately sprang up because they had no depth of earth. "But when the sun was up they were scorched, and because they had no root they withered away…But he who received the seed on stony places, this is he who hears the word immediately and receives it with joy; yet he has no root in himself, but endures only for a while. For when tribulation or persecution arise because of the word, immediately he stumbles" (13: 5-6, 20-21).

Here is another type of soil that prevents people from taking root spiritually. Satan uses tribulation or persecution, where there is not much earth, to defer the Word of God from the hearts of those who hear. This person is also in danger of going to hell straight from the church.

The third soil or heart is *the thorns*: "And some fell among thorns, and the thorns sprang up and choked them...Now he who received seed among the thorns is he who hears the word, and the cares of this world and the deceitfulness of riches choke the word, and he becomes unfruitful" (13:7, 22).

These Bible verses describe Satan using anxiety, worry due to the pressures of the world, and the deceitfulness of riches or worldly gain to defer the Word of God from the hearts of those who hear. He does this by choking it out of them, which can and will prevent people from getting saved and they also could end up going to hell straight from the church. Sadly, in the first three soils or hearts, all these people miss heaven by approximately one foot—the distance of the Word moving from one's head to one's heart.

The fourth and final soil or heart is *the good ground*: "But others fell on good ground and yielded a crop: some a hundredfold, some sixty, some thirty. He who has ears to hear, let him hear!...But he who received seed on the good ground is he who hears the word and understands it, who indeed bears fruit and produce: some a hundred, some sixty, some thirty" (13: 8-9, 23).

Satan is unable to defer the Word of God from the hearts of those who hear the Word on good ground. This is because they understand the Word and receive it. Satan will try his best to disrupt their spiritual growth, but these people will persevere, and they will *not* go to hell straight from the church.

When we look at these verses of Scripture describing human hearts hearing God's Word by the wayside, on stony places, and in the thorns, we must remember that these people did not hear the Word a single time. They hear or continue to hear the Word of God regularly. Even pastors and teachers regularly hear the very same Word that they teach to others. That is why pastors and teachers have such an awesome responsibility, and why the Bible tells us, "My brethren, let not many of you become teachers, knowing that we shall receive the stricter judgment" (James 3:1). Preachers and teachers of the Word are given more responsibility in sowing seeds on the different types of soils. They are without excuse and know better when it comes to salvation and the application of the Word. But no matter where one fits into the scheme of things, almost anyone can go to hell straight from the church if that is their desire. Everyone receives an invitation to come to heaven, but some have refused to RSVP by accepting Christ as personal Lord and Savior.

The Parable of the Sower and the Seed Chart

Four Types of Hearts

Wayside	**Stony Places**	**Thorns**	**Good Ground**
Not Saved	*Not Saved*	*Not Saved*	*Saved*
♥	♥	♥	♡
25%	*25%*	*25%*	*25% = 100%*
1/4	*1/4*	*1/4*	*1/4*

Results

Not Saved	*Saved*
	♡
75% = 3/4	*25% = 1/4*

The Parable of the Sower and the Seed Mathematical Breakdown

What does all this mean?

- *The amount of people who hear the Word of God in (for example) church is 100 out of 100.*
- *The amount of people who hear the Word of God in church and choose to get saved is 25 out of 100.*
- *The amount of people who hear the Word of God in church and choose not to get saved due to Satan's ability to defer the Word is 75 out of 100.*

Some disheartening statistics:

- *If there were 200 people in church, 150 of them would remain unsaved.*
- *If there were 300 people in church, 225 of them would remain unsaved.*
- *If there were 400 people in church, 300 of them would remain unsaved.*
- *If there were 500 people in church, 375 of them would remain unsaved.*
- *If there were 1,000 people in church, 750 of them would remain unsaved.*
- *If there were 10,000 people in church, 7,500 of them would remain unsaved.*

What this means is that many, many people could hear the Word of God regularly and still end up going to hell straight from the church. If that is true, one can only imagine the larger number of people who never get a chance to hear the Word regularly, or at all, who are dying and going to hell outside the church. We need to make absolutely certain we know Christ personally and are on our way to heaven. Once we know that for sure, in love, we need to make sure that the people in our circle of influence, inside and outside the local church, are sure that they are saved as well. When it comes to being held accountable by God in connection to Jesus Christ and salvation, the house of God is without excuse. As mentioned earlier, the Bible tells us in 1 Peter 4:17 that "For the time has come for judgment to begin at the house of God; and if it begins with us first, what will be the end be of those who do not obey the gospel of God?"

What will be the end of those who do not obey the gospel of God? The disturbing answer to this question is eternity in hell. We need to each make sure of our position in Christ to assure ourselves we are not going there, and especially not straight from the church.

CHAPTER EIGHT

The Trip Preliminaries: Setting the Stage

One Saturday, a megachurch in southern New Jersey was hosting a mission's conference, and all the churches from the Tri-State area were invited. Most churches attended. The conference started promptly at 8:00 AM with check-in and late registration in the lobby, where all the participants picked up their information packages for the day as they entered the church. After registration, people began filing into the sanctuary to enjoy a nice continental breakfast in the back before taking their seats and getting settled. At 9:00 AM praise and worship started in order to usher in the Spirit of the Lord. This part of the program lasted until about 9:25 AM. After that, the host for the event came forward to welcome everyone, thank them for coming, and then introduce the pastor of the church to those who did not know him. The pastor was going to be the first speaker and the one kicking off the general session.

The megachurch's pastor gave a powerful message on the need to share the gospel with a dark and dying world going to hell. His message sent a jumpstarting charge to the people and set the tone for the conference. The conference host then returned to the podium to lay out the schedule of the various workshops being offered and the classrooms where each would be held. Before dismissing everyone to their respective classes, she read the last workshop on the schedule. When she did, a murmur went across the room as people began whispering to those around them. The host said, "And the last workshop, 'A Field Trip to Hell,' will be held downstairs in classroom 666. It will be taught by Minister Kevin and Nikki Benton. You are dismissed." The attendees continued commenting on the workshop about hell. One person was even overheard saying, "I changed my mind and I think I'm going to the workshop about hell instead of the one I originally signed up for." After about five minutes, the hallways were clear as everyone arrived at their chosen workshops.

When my wife and I walked into our classroom with our Bibles, itineraries, handouts, and notes, we realized there were more people in there than had originally signed up on the pre-registration list. In fact, there were so many people in the room that many of them had to stand around the perimeter of the classroom. My brother, also in attendance, helped out by grabbing some chairs from the storage closet for those who did not have a seat. The class was now filled with sixty-eight people instead of the original twelve who had pre-registered. Once the class was settled, I introduced myself and my wife, and then my wife opened in prayer before we began.

I welcomed everyone and thanked them for coming to the workshop, and then I told them I would be their guide as we took a field trip to hell—a trip that would change their perspective for the rest of their lives. Before getting started, I addressed the important class preliminaries. I told the class I wanted to be sure that everyone there was a Christian. I asked if everyone in the classroom had received Jesus Christ as their personal Savior, and, if not, to please raise their hand so we could pray with them. My wife and I scanned the room looking for at least one hand to go up, but no hand was raised. So we assumed that everyone belonged to Christ, which was to our delight. Next, I passed out the itineraries and some handouts. After going through my protocol, my wife Nikki gave some background and historicity on the gospel of Luke, with a special focus on chapter sixteen, verses nineteen through thirty-one; the parable of the rich man and Lazarus. Nikki's main point was that the purpose of the book of Luke was to make it unequivocally clear that Jesus Christ is the Son of Man, who, by his resurrection, fulfilled his mission to seek and to save that which was lost. She emphasized that Luke showed that Christ was not only divine, but equally human. The gospel of Luke stresses the humanity and compassion of Jesus by devoting more of the writing to Christ's feelings than any of the other books in the Bible.

We then gave the breakdown of the book of Luke, which is broken into four parts: (1) introducing the Son of Man (1:1-4:13); (2) the ministry of the Son of Man (4:14-9:50); (3) the rejection of the Son of Man (9:51-19:27); and, (4) the crucifixion and the resurrection of the Son of Man (19:28-24:53). We gave a brief overview of the Scriptures leading up to our focal text for the day, and then we were ready to begin the workshop.

I told the workshop participants that the first thing I wanted to do was establish that the Word of God is the truth, the whole truth, and nothing but the truth. We need to resolve in our hearts that what we experience on our field trip to hell is real. We will soon see that it is not a place where you go in the afterlife to hang out and have a good time being with friends, as some of our misguided youth believe. The Bible establishes and confirms itself to be the truth in 2 Timothy 3:16-17, which says: "All Scripture is given by inspiration of God, and is profitable for doctrine, for reproof, for correction, for instruction in righteousness, that the man of God may be complete, thoroughly equipped for every good work." I further defined our purpose for the day by telling everyone that our fieldtrip would be a trip away from the classroom to permit the gathering of data at firsthand. After that, I identified the two men's lives that we would be examining on our trip.

The Rich Man and Lazarus

Luke 16:19-31 gives us a contrast between the rich man and Lazarus. Verse nineteen says "There was a certain rich man who was clothed in purple (which represents costly or royal garments) and fine linen and fared sumptuously every day." Of course this man had a lot of money. He was most likely very popular, had a lot of friends, and probably wore the best designer fashions. If there were the latest model cars back then, he had them, along with a few houses with gates all around. In short, he had all the material gain one could ever want. Many men and women attending church on Sunday are the same way. And even though they are wealthy, they are just as spiritually bankrupt as was the rich man from the Luke parable. On the other hand, verses twenty and twenty-one tell us about another gentleman by the name of Lazarus who was a diseased beggar. "But there was a certain beggar named Lazarus, full of sores, who laid at his gate, desiring to be fed with the crumbs which fell from the rich man's table. Moreover the dogs came and licked his sores." This parable clearly conveys the beggar's present afflicted condition, but at the same time it also shows the rich man's apparent carelessness.

The beggar also represents many people we come in contact with, both inside and outside the church. He was more than likely looked down upon, despised and rejected in society, and neglected in the church. Perhaps he had a sickly look, a foul smell, and dirty attire. Today, this man would be found digging in trash cans trying to find something to eat. Or he would sit and beg and hope that compassion would move someone's heart, causing them to spare him some change to get something to eat, which would be the highlight of his day. Most of us would pretend we did not see him or know of his unfortunate situation, and we would pass by the beggar. According to the parable, the rich man did not even give Lazarus the crumbs that fell from his table.

The conclusion of both lives is revealed in Luke 16:22-26, which says "So it was that the beggar died, and was carried by the angels to Abraham's Bosom. The rich man also died and was buried. And being in torments in Hades, he lifted up his eyes and saw Abraham afar off, and Lazarus in his bosom. "Then he cried and said, 'Father Abraham, have mercy on me, and send Lazarus that he may dip the tip of his finger in water and cool my tongue; for I am tormented in this flame.' But Abraham said, 'Son, remember that in your lifetime you received your good things, and likewise Lazarus evil things; but now he is comforted and you are tormented. And besides all this, between us and you there is a great gulf fixed, so that those who want to pass from here to you cannot, nor can those from there pass to us.'"

Abraham's Bosom

Abraham's Bosom was an abode like heaven. It was a place of honor and comfort for the righteous dead. Abraham's Bosom was where the Old Testament saints stayed until after Jesus Christ's death, burial, and resurrection. Before he arose, Jesus went down in to Abraham's Bosom and preached to the Old Testament saints that they might receive a special provision. After the Lord rose from the dead, these saints were offered the blessing of going to the third heaven into the presence of God's throne, and it is where today's saints who have placed their faith in Jesus' finished work will go one day when this life is over. One way to look at this is that the non-Christian saints of the Old Testament were rescued on credit based on what Jesus would eventually do as a result of sacrificing himself on the cross. Abraham's Bosom is the comforting place created by God that was in close proximity of the suffering place of torments called hell.

When the rich man died and was buried, he was sent into the torments of Hades—a place for the unrighteous dead. In this case, Hades (or hell) was clearly a place of torments characterized primarily by fire. The rich man can see Lazarus in Abraham's Bosom, but he cannot get there because a great chasm between the two places prevents passage from one place to the other.

Matthew 12:40 reads, "For as Jonah was three days and three nights in the belly of the great fish, so will the Son of Man be three days and three nights in the heart of the earth." This Scripture indicates that the location of hell is in the heart of the earth, which we discuss in more detail shortly. And since Abraham's Bosom is in close proximity to hell, it too is in the heart of the earth. Once again, Abraham's Bosom is not heaven per se, but it is a place of comfort created by God which is like heaven for the unsaved Old Testament saints until after the death, burial, and resurrection of Israel's Messiah. Once Messiah Jesus rose from the dead, the Old Testament saints went to the third heaven into the presence of God's throne. For this to happen, however, Jesus had to rise from death after three days in order to fulfill the prophecy in the gospel of John, which says, "Jesus answered and said to them, 'Destroy this temple (talking about Himself), and in three days I will raise it up'" (2:19).

The Lord spent three days and three nights in hell. While he was there he picked Satan up with one hand and with the other hand he took the keys to death, hell, and the grave, assuring victory for all believers. This was also important for the Old Testament saints who were in Abraham's Bosom because it assured victory for them, as well. As mentioned earlier, it was after the Lord spent three nights in the heart of the earth and was resurrected that they were able to go to the third heaven—God's throne in the sky.

Death is the Equalizer of Persons

Hell, then, is located in the heart of the earth. Besides Matthew 12:40, another confirmation of hell's location is Ephesians 4:9, which reads, "Now this, *'He ascended'*—what does it mean but that He also first descended into the lower parts of the earth?" The heart of the earth and the lower parts of the earth represent the same place. Further, Revelation 20:10 assures us that "The devil, who deceived them, was cast into the lake of fire and brimstone where the beast and the false prophet are. And they will be tormented day and night forever and ever." This verse says that hell consists of fire and brimstone, which is located at the center or core of the earth where hot molten lava is found. Hot molten lava consists of fire and brimstone. Many scientists believe and have agreed that the center of the earth is approximately 12,000 to 13,000 degrees Fahrenheit. The temperature of the inner core of the earth is approximately 5,000 to 6,000 degrees Centigrade, which is comparable to the surface of the sun where the photosphere ranges anywhere from 5,500 degrees Centigrade to 6,000 degrees Centigrade. This means that the temperature of the lower part of the earth is about the same as the temperature of the surface of the sun. So we know that it must be very, very hot.

Looking at the round earth from a two-dimensional standpoint, no matter where one is positioned, the heart and lowest part of earth will always be the core or the center of it. For example, if I live at the top of the earth's sphere in, say, China, the heart and lower part of the earth will be the core or center. If I lived at the bottom of the earth's sphere in Brazil, the heart and lower part of the earth would still be the core or the center. This would be true whether I lived in the western hemisphere of the earth or in the eastern hemisphere. The heart and lower part of the earth would be at the core or center. No matter where I was on the face of the globe, I could descend to the heart or lowest part of the earth and end up in the same place. The approximate distance from the earth's surface to the heart of the earth would be 37,000 feet or 8 to 10 miles deep. In the movie *Ghost*, hell is depicted as a place underground as well. The character Carl Burner (an appropriate name, to say the least), played by actor Tony Goldwyn, gets hit by a car and dies. The demons then come out from underground, grab his spirit, and drag him down the street and eventually back underground where he would end up going to hell and burning. Hollywood definitely got this part right, because hell is located in the lower parts or center of the earth.

The beggar, in the parable of the rich man and Lazarus, died and was basically forgotten on this side of life. The rich man, on the other hand, died and probably had a very luxurious home-going service. Despite their different funeral arrangements, however, the important thing to realize is that *death is a great equalizer and no respecter of persons.* Death is not limited to a specific race, religion, education level, socioeconomic status, age, gender, height, weight, or anything else, and at some point in time it applies to everyone. Death is an unavoidable reality of life. Death also forces us to deal with the afterlife question. Will we see our loved ones again? Are they in a better place? Are they in heaven? The truth is that not everyone will go to heaven. I am almost certain that the rich man's friends and neighbors assumed he would be in heaven when he died. But that is not what the parable says. If he could have traded places with the beggar, he would have, but no amount of fame or fortune could have helped that poor soul.

Now it is time to cross over and begin our tour of hell. My readers will not be harmed, but we will witness things unlike we have ever seen before—things that can have a trying psychological and emotional affect. I just need everyone to stay together, remain very quiet, follow me, and open their Bibles to Luke 16:19-31.

CHAPTER NINE

A Field Trip to Hell: The Blessed Side of Regret

In my workshop at the megachurch, everyone was opening their Bibles to Luke 16:19-31, the parable of the rich man and Lazarus. Suddenly, the lights in the classroom slowly dimmed as people began looking around. Eventually, as the light grew dimmer and dimmer, the room went pitch-black. I was wearing a black suit, and I was seemingly disappearing into the background. The seminar room was now so dark that no one could see their hand an inch in front of their face. The participants began discussing the situation. Some wondered if a fuse had blown, or if the church's electric bill had not been paid.

All of the sudden everyone screamed in horror as we began to descend downward very quickly until coming to a complete stop. It was still very, very dark. But then, in the midst of darkness, a faint light began to appear from a large lit fire pit. Everyone was now standing on the side of Abraham's Bosom. The look on everyone's face was one of shock and fear, as if they were asking, "How did we get here? Where are we? What is this place?"

I turned to the crowd and told them, "Everyone just relax. I know, I know. You are surprised. I tried to tell you. We have now arrived in hell." Once again instructing everyone, I said, "Now remember to stay together and keep very quiet. And follow me as we begin to look at the characteristics of this place."

"If you look to your left in verse 23a, it says, *'And being in torments in Hades.'* This word *torments* is plural, which implies that there is more than just the torment of the universally known burning fire. The flames are traditionally the only aspect of hell that tends to be referenced when it is mentioned. On the other hand, hell is characteristic of at least thirty individual different types of torments that go on simultaneously. Some torments are added to the list because they can be justifiably suggested within the scope of what the Bible states or implies. More than that, the scary part is that there may be even more torment here, as hell is not only the ultimate place of limitless suffering, but a vast mystery to grasp and behold. The last time I checked, one torment alone was bad enough, but thirty or more going on at the same time for eternity is definitely a 'hell' of a situation. Some torments are reproduced more than once but for different reasons, making it a torment in and of itself. This is the place of ultimate spiritual, mental, emotional, and physical pain and suffering. It is the ultimate place of irritation, agitation, loneliness, and frustration in every sense of the word. To sum it up, as I just mentioned, all the torments in hell fit into these four categories which are spiritual pain and suffering, mental pain and suffering, emotional pain and suffering, and of course physical or bodily pain and suffering. To add to that, there will be specific sufferings, and sometimes more than one, in the areas of the five senses: sight, hearing, taste, touch, and smell."

The First Torment

"If you step this way, the next part of that same Scripture, verse 23b, says, *'he lifted up his eyes,'* which implies that in hell people have a sense of sight. In hell, the sense of sight is the first torment. In Isaiah 66:24, the Bible describes exactly what people will see: 'And they shall go forth and look upon the corpses of the men who have transgressed against Me. For their worm does not die, and their fire is not quenched. They shall be an abhorrence to all flesh.'

This is graphic and scary; it looks like dead bodies or corpses being eaten up by worms and being burned at the same time. The worms and the fire are separate but inclusive torments. To add to that, our sense of sight will greatly impact our minds and emotions due to the nature of the horrific sights that will be continually seen for eternity. This also implies that down here we will not only have the sense of sight, but we will also be able to feel the negative emotions of anxiety, fear, and trepidation, which are emotional sufferings or torments. Keep in mind that at the end of the verse in Isaiah 66:24, we read that *'They shall be abhorrence to all flesh.'* The word *abhor* means to turn aside from, or to keep away from. It has the sense of turning aside in scorn, or shuddering in fear at the horrific sight of people being tormented over and over and over again.

"This torment and every other torment experienced here in hell will happen over and over without being able to die because people in hell are already physically dead. The suffering is never-ending and the pain is inescapable. There is nowhere to turn; this is the final destination. There will be no possibility of closing your eyes or running and hiding—because everywhere you turn you see hell. Do you remember when you were little and a sibling or friend was playing around and jumping out from behind something in a disguise? Do you remember screaming? Or that it almost scared you half to death, and that your heart skipped a few beats as you gasped for air because of what you saw? Inhabitants in hell will experience this fright at unimaginable levels for eternity. In hell, no one has the luxury of calming down to get themselves together. The sights and torments will cause you to feel like you are having cardiac arrest—which is the second torment in hell."

The Second Torment

"Luke 21:25-33 talks about the second coming of Christ, when he returns to judge the world. Verse 26 tells us how humankind is going to be affected when he comes: *'Men's hearts failing them from fear and the expectation of those things which are coming on the earth, for the powers of the heavens will be shaken.'* How does this apply to hell? Notice that men's hearts are failing because of fear and the expectation of those things which are coming. If their hearts would fail from fear in this context, how much more will their hearts fail from fear in the ultimate place of fear, the place that is the most unimaginable place of fear and torment? Whatever level of pain and suffering that can be imagined will be infinitely worse in hell. And all of this without the possibility of ending it all, for there is no death. Let's move along. Follow me.

The Third Torment

"The third torment in hell deals with a bothersome sight that invokes the painful emotion of regret. Like the rich man, many in hell will see heaven from afar and realize they should have given their hearts to Jesus during their short time on earth. Matthew 19:23 says, *'Then Jesus said to his disciples, 'Assuredly, I say to you that it is hard for a rich man to enter the kingdom of heaven. And again I say to you, it is easier for a camel to go through the eye of a needle than for a rich man to enter into the kingdom of God."* There is nothing wrong with having possessions, but when our possessions possess us to the point where we see no need for Jesus or salvation, that is a problem of major proportions. Matthew 16:26 says, *'For what profit is it to a man if he gains the whole world, and loses his own soul? Or what will a man give in exchange for his soul?'* Keep in mind that we are just visiting as tourists, but for this rich man and everyone else here, it is too late. They are able to see Abraham afar off and Lazarus in his bosom. Lazarus is also a painful symbol and a constant reminder that invokes emotional regret."

Giving an example, I said, "Have you ever made a mistake in life that caused you the emotional pain of regret, and then had to come across something or somebody that was a painful reminder of the mistake you made? With all the negative painful emotions that came with the mistake, there is also the pain of desiring to turn back the hands of time so you could make a better or different decision. But alas, it is too late. Now imagine this emotional pain at an infinite and eternal level. That is what the rich man was experiencing as he looked at Lazarus in Abraham's Bosom. The painful emotion of regret brings with it recognition, comprehension, understanding, and realization. The pain of emotional regret is brought by a visual reminder that lasts for all of eternity. All those in hell will have in common seeing a sight that brings them the pain of regret."

The Fourth Torment

"If you look and listen closely you can hear the rich man crying. Notice in Luke 16:24a it says, *'Then he cried and said, 'Father Abraham, have mercy on me.''* The rich man crying reveals the fourth torment of hell. He is crying out because of all the spiritual, mental, emotional, and physical suffering he is simultaneously experiencing. The suffering and pain is unimaginable and unbearable, and there is no stopping it and no way out of it. It is the final destination of the unrighteous.

"If I could have your attention and elaborate here for a second, the rich man crying in the context of hell denotes three things. The *first* is physiological crying, meaning tears and an emotional release. The *second* is crying out to the Lord in prayer for help. While we are on this point, it is amazing how religiosity goes out the window when people are in trouble. Some of the most effective prayers we ever pray are the shortest and the ones that get right to the point. I know. I have prayed a few Lord-have-mercy prayers throughout my life. The *third* is a loud expression of grief as if to be mourning for the dead. All three of these meanings apply to the rich man and everybody else existing here in the unfortunate situation of hell.

"Crying out to Father Abraham also implies that in hell one can talk, and that means that one can breathe, though barely. It is interesting, however, that the rich man is expressing himself in the form of a prayer. It may be surprising to hear, but the largest prayer meeting ever assembled is going on right here in hell, and it will be a prayer meeting that lasts for all eternity. No matter what anyone's religious orientation was on earth, everyone here is now a believer. They have no doubts this is a real place. The atheists also are now convinced of the reality of this place, and even they are praying. They would love another chance to receive Jesus Christ as their personal Savior, but now it is too late. There aren't any more atheists in hell."

The Fifth Torment

I continued addressing the tour group: "Those we hear praying their hearts out like never before, including the rich man, have only torment to look forward to. Part of that torment will be the pain of unanswered prayers. And that pain is the fifth torment. The Bible says in Proverbs that *'Hope deferred makes the heart sick, But when the desire comes, it is a tree of life'* (13:12).

"The heart being sick refers not only to physical sickness but emotional states of loneliness, depression, discouragement, despair, sadness, and sorrow. Have you ever prayed and hoped for something you believed in your heart of hearts was God's will? For whatever reason, due to God's sovereign choice, he chose not to answer that prayer, or at least he did not answer it the way you wanted. Your perceived rejection made you feel abandoned by God, making you feel all alone, depressed, discouraged, and in despair. But later you found out that God knew what was best for you. At that time, however, the perceived rejection made your heart feel burdened. Along with all the other torments, this is what the rich man and others here are experiencing. It is continuous, unanswered prayers, and the heart sickness that comes with the hope of escaping this place."

The Sixth Torment

"Next, the rich man is about to make a request of Father Abraham, which is shown in Luke 16:24b: *'Father Abraham, ...send Lazarus that he may dip the tip of his finger in water and cool my tongue; for I am tormented in this flame.'* This is the sixth torment, the painful suffering of a hot, dry tongue, mouth, and throat, bringing the agonizing pain of thirstiness. What this means is that inhabitants of hell will retain their sense of taste." I gave the group two examples: "Have you ever tried to swallow hot coffee, hot chocolate, or hot tea a little bit too soon? As you sipped it, it burned your tongue and your throat, not to mention turning your tongue white on the burned area. Or have you ever gone jogging on a hot summer day and the longer the distance you jogged the more your mouth and throat became very painfully dry? Trying to maintain proper breathing while running, you tried to swallow air and your throat began to hurt. The only thing at that point that was on your mind was getting an ice cold glass of water to quench your painful thirst. Now imagine experiencing that kind of continuous pain and suffering at an infinite level for eternity, and never being able to quench your thirst or soothe the pain. This is what the rich man and others here are experiencing, along with all the other torments."

The Seventh and Eighth Torments

I turned to the crowd of tourists again and said, "I would like to suggest that if the torment of thirstiness, which is a physiological need, exists here in hell, then other painful physiological needs must also exist here as well. I would like to suggest that the torments of hunger and sleep deprivation are the seventh and eighth torments of hell. Those in hell will not be able to satisfy these needs, and there will be starvation and lack of rest for the rest of their days. The Bible does not specifically talk about the torment of hunger down here, but it does mention the torment of sleep deprivation in Revelation 14:9-11: *'And the smoke of their torment ascends forever and ever;* ***and they have no rest day and night.'***

"If sleep deprivation and the horrible, unending pain of thirstiness exist in hell, I think that it would be safe to suggest that starvation does as well. At a minimum, we all can identify with what it feels like to be so painfully hungry our stomach growls, and so tired we are completely burned out (no pun intended)."

The Ninth Torment

I gave another example as I continued addressing the tourists in hell: "Speaking of being dead tired, have you ever gotten inside of a sauna for a while and after you got out, due to the heat level, you just felt drained? This brings us to the ninth torment of hell—heat exhaustion and weakness from fatigue, due to the unbearable level of heat. After some time in the sauna, all you want to do is eat and get some sleep. Psalm 88:4 says, 'I am counted with those who go down to the pit; I am like a man who has no strength.' These agonizing and never-ending torments at an infinite level are what it would be like in hell. Note that the rich man is asking Father Abraham to send Lazarus to give him some water. He is asking for the very person he rejected and refused to provide with the crumbs off his table. We can learn from this. You never know when you might need the very people you reject from day to day, so remember this parable and treat everyone back on earth with the love of Jesus Christ."

The Tenth Torment

I told the tour group that the last thing we would examine at this point before moving along is the words of the rich man, *"for I am tormented in this flame"* (Luke 16:24). "So now we finally get to the torment of the traditionally and universally known aspect of hell, the fiery flames, which is the tenth torment. The fiery flames cause burning, for we can see that the rich man is on fire. The fire down here will never be extinguished as it is unquenchable. Mark 9:44b says: *'And the fire is not quenched.'"*

Being tormented by the flames of hell means you will have your sense of feeling. When the rich man said *"I am tormented,"* I felt this must be given special attention.

Turning to the crowd to elaborate, I said, "The phrase *'I am'* is in the present tense; it means 'I am *currently* tormented.' Whatever is mentioned after the phrase 'I am' qualifies the statement. The rich man in the parable said he was being tormented; he was being tormented in the present, and always in the process of being in the present. If I said, 'I am from Philadelphia,' I will, in the present and always in the process of being in the present, be from Philadelphia. Even if I move to Delaware, I am still from Philadelphia, because that is where I was born. Even if I lied about where I am from, I will still, in the present, always be in the process of being from Philadelphia. The reason is that time and history solidified that fact as truth. I can also try to convince myself that I'm from another place if I choose not to accept my grassroots origin, but the truth of the matter is that Philadelphia is where I am really from. Now I might say that I am skinny. Something like that can change over time, depending on my exercise and eating habits. In the case of the rich man and all those who join him here in hell, their situation cannot change because he has said *'I am tormented,'* which means he is in the present and is always in the process of being in the present—*tormented.* Nothing can change for him or the others.

"The word *tormented* the rich man used to describe himself also shows present tense. He said he was tormented *in this flame*, which has an obvious eternal implication to it. In other words, the rich man and the others here in hell will, in the present and always in the process of being in the present, be tormented by this flame—and the twenty-nine other torments that accompany it.

"Have you ever touched a hot pan or iron by accident? Why was that feeling so painful? This process happened when your hand touched the hot pan or iron: the signal or electrical impulse traveled from neuron to neuron across synapses until the message got to your brain, which told you to move your hand quickly. That reflex was done without you even having to think about it. This process happens when the electrical impulse starts out in the nerve endings inside of the finger or hand at the neuron dendrites, which are finger-like extensions located at the end of the neuron. Then the impulse travels down the neuron arm, which is called the axon. Once the message continues to the inter neuron in the cross section of the spinal cord, it alerts the brain of danger and excites the motor neuron. The terminal buttons of the motor neuron then release a chemical called a neurotransmitter. The muscle cells then contract causing the hand to move away from the hot pan or iron. This signal moves at 224 miles per hour!

"It would be hard to imagine that painful feeling multiplied to an infinite degree all over one's body as it burns in this flame. Yet that is what the rich man is experiencing. It will be forever, and the sufferer cannot die or escape. Once this field trip is over and we return to our respective homes and day-to-day lives on earth, the rich man and all the others occupying hell will still be tormented by this continuous and everlasting flame."

The Eleventh Torment

I was not finished with this line of reasoning, so I turned to the group of tourists and continued. "In addition to this, the eternal flames will bring an awful toxic stench from what is burning, and this leads us to torment number eleven. Satan and his demons will eventually burn in hell, along with all the people on earth who died and rejected Jesus Christ by not receiving him as their personal Savior. One can only form a weak mental image of the unimaginable wretched stench that will pervade the underworld. All of this means that those in hell will also have their sense of smell, and that they will be tormented for all eternity with this terrible and offensive odor."

The Twelfth and Thirteenth Torments

"If those in hell retain their sense of smell, then the extremely unpleasant scent will bring a twelfth and thirteenth torment, that of having a nauseated feeling and a queasy, upset stomach because of breathing the unbearable stench." I wanted to elaborate: "The unbearable stench here will cause the feeling of nausea and a queasy, upset stomach as they both normally go hand in hand. But they are separate torments in and of themselves because both individually can have a negative effect on a person without the other, and each can cause pain and discomfort." Continuing to elaborate, "For example, I can feel nauseated without having an upset stomach, and I can have an upset stomach without feeling nauseated. Both together and each separately can make me sick. The burning stench of those sent to hell, along with Satan and his demons, will never cease." I turned to the crowd and gave an example of what this would be like: "Have you ever walked by a trash dumpster on a hot summer day and experienced the stench of garbage? Maybe you tried covering your nose and mouth as your face frowned up, but you probably still felt queasy and dizzy. A smell like that could cause someone to regurgitate their lunch. In hell, that pain and suffering will go on without relent, and that queasy and nauseated feeling will never let up. Nor will there ever be any breath of fresh air for eternity."

The Fourteenth Torment

"While we are on the subject of the stomach," I said, "that brings us to the fourteenth torment of hell—the fear of falling forever as we briefly experienced on our way here. This fear can affect one's breathing and the stomach, and so it has a physical element to the torment. But it can also have enormous psychological aspects. One of the names for hell in Scripture is the "bottomless pit," which suggests the fearful torment of the feeling of falling forever. In the book of Revelation, Jesus comes down from heaven during the tribulation period, picks Satan up, and binds him up in the great chain for one thousand years. Then he casts Satan into the bottomless pit. Revelation 20:3 specifically says, *'And he cast him into the bottomless pit, and shut him up, and set a seal on him, so that he should deceive the nations no more till the thousand years were finished. But after these things he must be released for a little while.'*"

I gave the tourists an example of the feeling of falling forever by saying, "On earth, have you ever been on an airplane when the plane was flying very smoothly and then all of a sudden it hit an unexpected air pocket due to turbulence? The sudden drop downward brings the fear of the plane falling out of the sky, with death being inescapable. This psychologically tormenting experience has been known to give passengers high anxiety and panic attacks, and it causes them to sweat profusely and even close the window shade and pray. In some cases people have even been known to suffer heart complications. Imagine how unimaginatively worse this type of experience would be for eternity."

The Fifteenth Torment

It was now time to elaborate on the other torments in hell closely related to the torment of the psychological fear of falling forever. I addressed the group and said, "There is another stomach torment down here that is tied to the tormenting psychological fear of falling forever, but must be put in a category by itself. This brings us to the fifteenth torment, the feeling of falling. Have you ever gotten on a roller coaster with a stomach-squeezing drop? These rides take you straight up about three stories high and then they drop you. The drop seems to last a lifetime, and during and right after the fall it is difficult to catch one's breath. The fearful feeling we get in our stomach is fun and exciting because the drop tends to last only a few seconds. Many people enjoy the feeling of fear as long as it occurs under controlled circumstances. The idea of falling sometimes makes us sick to the point of feeling like we are going to vomit. Sometimes when we go on rides like that the first thing we say when we get off is 'I'm not getting on that ride anymore.' A drop that is safe and controlled and that lasts only a few seconds is one thing. But a fall that lasts for eternity without any safety or control would be infinitely tormenting. Hell is no amusement park, and whatever level of pain and fear you can imagine, the sense of falling in hell will be unimaginably worse."

The Sixteenth Torment

Getting back to my original point, which was the flames, I stated, "Also, in connection with the torments of the flames and the smell from what is burning, there is, as we can all see, the thick black smoke produced from it all. As you already know on earth, people die in house fires all the time from smoke inhalation when the actual flames of the fire never even touch them. When we talked about the rich man crying, I told you this implied that in hell you can talk as well as breathe. Focusing in on breathing part, this brings us to torment number sixteen—coughing and choking from smoke inhalation. Right now their lungs are filling with the black smoke, but they cannot die because their spirits are immortal. Revelation 14:9-13 talks about the announcement of the Three Angels during the tribulation period. The last announcement made by the third angel talks about anyone who worships the beast and his image being tormented in fire and brimstone in the presence of angels and Jesus the Lamb, right here in hell. Verse eleven specifically references the smoke from hell due to all those who are burning. It reads, ***'And the smoke of their torment ascends forever and ever;*** *and they have no rest day or night, who worship the beast and his image, and whoever receives the mark of his name.'"*

The Seventeenth Torment

"Another torment in and of itself can be suggested along with choking, and that would be the seventeenth torment—eyes burning from the smoke. Those suffering in hell will be tormented by breathing the smoke, which is what causes burning eyes, coughing, choking, and experiencing the irritation of the filthy air." I then gave them another Scripture commenting on the nature of the air in hell: Revelation 9:2. *"And he opened the bottomless pit,* ***and smoke arose out of the pit like the smoke of a great furnace.*** *So the sun and the air were darkened because of the smoke of the pit."*

Trying to give the people following me on the tour the Scripture in its proper context, I said, "Once again this is talking about the tribulation period on earth, but notice where the smoke is coming from. It is coming out from right here in the bottomless pit of hell. I tend to have a hard time breathing and seeing at family barbecues back on earth when my uncle sometimes burns the food on the grill. I find myself covering my nose at the smell of burned chicken wings and coughing and choking and wiping my irritated eyes due to the smoke from it all. I cannot even begin to fathom experiencing that kind of unending suffering."

The Eighteenth Torment

No one said anything because of the shock at what they were learning. I then told them we were going to move forward and a little closer to where Father Abraham is, and to follow me and stay together. Arriving at our next position, I pointed up at Father Abraham. "If you look up to your left to see where the rich man was looking, you will see in Luke 16:23 Father Abraham and Lazarus in his bosom. *'And being in torments in Hades, he lifted up his eyes and saw Abraham afar off, and Lazarus in his bosom.'* Father Abraham is about to respond to the rich man, so let's listen in on the conversation in verse twenty-five, which says, *'But Abraham said, 'Son, remember that in your lifetime you received your good things, and likewise Lazarus evil things; but now he is comforted and you are tormented.''* Once again, this confirms there will be the ability to talk here in hell. But now we learn there will also be the ability to remember or recall events from memory on earth, which is the eighteenth torment in hell. Erwin Lutzer, a well respected pastor and biblical scholar, once said of hell, 'You will have extremely heightened perception and much keener understanding.' Those consigned to hell will remember the so-called good life they had without Jesus. They will remember all the people they should have treated well and did not. They will remember all the opportunities to come to Christ in faith but did not. They will remember all the people who tried to direct them to faith in Christ but whom they ignored. Most of all, if you should go to hell yourselves, you will remember that you actually visited this place by joining us on this field trip."

One of the ladies on the tour raised her hand and asked a question, as Mr. Theo Turner, another participant, looked on intently as if to be searching to hear what she would ask. It was the sweet Ms. Helen Pitts, who kind of resembled my grandmother, who was standing next to my sister Tamika in the back of the crowd. She asked, "I know we are not being affected by the torments, except a little bit psychologically and emotionally, but with all the torments down here, why doesn't the rich man just go out of his mind and become insane?" My sister answered the question. "God is keeping the rich man and everyone here in their right mind because if they were not, that would be an escape from some of the psychological and emotional sufferings. Keep in mind that this is the ultimate place of spiritual, mental, emotional, and physical pain."

Continuing on with my elaboration, I remarked, "Ultimately, your personal memories will bring you eternal regret, mental and emotional pain and suffering, and they will even get you upset and angry at yourself. You will be angry at yourself because you will want to have many of those precious moments back to receive Jesus, so that you could ensure a different outcome than the one that led to the place where you are. But it will be too late, and like the rich man, you will have to live with that fact forever." I drew everyone's attention back to Lazarus, who is in Father Abraham's Bosom, because I wanted to stress what Abraham said to the rich man: '*"But now he is comforted and you are tormented.'* The use of the word *now* refers to Lazarus being comforted right now, at this immediate time. It also refers to the rich man being tormented right now. This is another confirmation of how the pain and suffering down here is always in the present tense. For all of us who are rescued from this circumstance, we will be comforted in the life to come no matter what has happened to us in the present life back on earth. This is what gives us hope. The rich man and others here with him have no such hope, nor will they ever have such hope."

The Nineteenth Torment

My disposition changed as I prepared for the next part of the tour. I told the tour group, "I really need you to pay close attention as you view this next part of the tour because it is the most important part of our trip." After walking for a few minutes, they noticed a dim light beginning to slowly but surely get brighter and brighter as they got closer to its source. After walking a little more, with the light getting brighter and brighter, we arrived at our next stopping point. I told them, "Please make sure that you can see this next part and if you can't, please move to a position where you can." Then I turned and addressed the throng: "If you look very closely in between where the rich man is down there and where Father Abraham and Lazarus are up there, you will see a fiery chasm. Now listen carefully because Father Abraham is about to speak again. In Luke 16:26 he says, *'And besides all this, between us and you there is a great gulf fixed, so that those who want to pass from here to you cannot, nor can those from there pass to us.'"*

Elaborating on what was just said, I turned to the crowd and declared, "The phrase *'And besides all this,'* means that everything we have just discussed prior to this statement and everything we will discuss after this statement do not reveal the worst aspects of hell. The worst part of this place is that not only is there no passage back and forth from heaven to hell, or from hell to heaven, but because of the fiery chasm, the spiritual pain and suffering the rich man and everybody else is experiencing makes them totally separated from the presence of God for eternity. This is the nineteenth torment, and it is the worst torment of them all. Being eternally separated from God is also called the second death, as explained in 2 Thessalonians 1:9: *'These shall be punished with everlasting destruction from the presence of the Lord and from the glory of His power.'*

"Another Bible verse confirming that separation from God is the second death is found in Revelation 21:8, which says: *'But the cowardly, unbelieving, abominable, murderers, sexually immoral, sorcerers, idolaters, and all liars shall have their part in the lake which burns with fire and brimstone, which is the second death.'*" I wanted to explain further. "This is the second spiritual death because whenever anything is separated or cut off from that to which it belongs, it ends up dying. For example, if you separate a fish from the water, it eventually dies. If you separate plants from the ground, they eventually die. It is the same with human beings separated from God, because it is in God that *'we live and move and have our being'* as stated in Acts 17:28. When a man or woman is separated down here in hell from the God who gives them life, they die again. For fish, water is a necessity, not an option. The same thing applies to the ground for plants. Equally so, God is not an option for his human creation; he is a necessity. Or else man and woman will die again."

The Twentieth Torment

I continued to develop this thinking further: "In conjunction with that torment, now that the presence of God is no longer here in hell, this brings us to the twentieth torment, the terror and fear due to the free flowing presence of continuous death and evil. Psalm 73:18-19 says, *'Surely You set them in slippery places; You cast them down to destruction. Oh, how they are brought to desolation, as in a moment! They are utterly consumed with terrors.'* Since God is love, and since God's presence is gone, that means that love is gone. Since perfect love casts out fear, and since love is gone, now fear is present. This fear involves torment. 1 John 4:18 says, *'There is no fear in love; but perfect love casts out fear, because fear involves torment.'* In hell, evil has no limits or restrictions as on earth where God's presence abides because of his children. This evil in hell will cause overwhelming terror, fear, and trepidation because of being surrounded on every side by continuous death and the presence of darkness for all eternity. In 2 Samuel 22:5-6, we read, *'When the waves of death surrounded me, the floods of ungodliness made me afraid. The sorrows of Sheol surrounded me; the snares of death confronted me.'*

"On earth, do you remember watching a scary movie? And in the movie there was a lady running from the killer, but she fell down while being chased? She always managed to get away and hide somewhere in the house, right? But the sheer terror of knowing that the killer was somewhere present in the house made the hair on the back of your neck stand up. Besides knowing she could be killed, even though neither she nor the audience knew where the killer was, he would pop out of nowhere, standing right behind her with a large knife in his hands. When she realized it was him, there were screams of horror and, usually, a very bad ending for her. Now take that feeling of stark danger and think of what it would be like down here for eternity without the presence of God."

The Twenty-First Torment

"Even though all of us on this field trip to hell can see what it looks like down here, a lot of people back on earth wonder about its appearance. When you get back to earth, tell them that the best description of hell is found in Luke 16:23-31."

> *And being in torments in Hades, he lifted up his eyes and saw Abraham afar off, and Lazarus in his bosom. "Then he cried and said, 'Father Abraham, have mercy on me, and send Lazarus that he may dip the tip of his finger in water and cool my tongue; for I am tormented in this flame.' But Abraham said, 'Son, remember that in your lifetime you received your good things, and likewise Lazarus evil things; but now he is comforted and you are tormented. And besides all this, between us and you there is a great gulf fixed, so that those who want to pass from here to you cannot, nor can those from there pass to us.' Then he said, 'I beg you therefore, father, that you would send him to my father's house, for I have five brothers, that he may testify to them, lest they also come to this place of torment.' Abraham said to him, 'They have Moses*

and the prophets; let them hear them.' And he said, 'No, father Abraham; but if one goes to them from the dead, they will repent.' But he said to him, 'If they do not hear Moses and the prophets, neither will they be persuaded though one rise from the dead.'"

"Tell them to keep in mind that the locations of these two places—hell and the bosom of Abraham—are in close proximity because the rich man and Lazarus are able to have a conversation, and both are located in the heart of the earth. More importantly, as it pertains to Abraham's Bosom, let them know that it is a place of comfort for the righteous dead which has been created by God, despite being in the core of the earth, so therefore no harm will come to them. Luke 16:23 says, *'And being in torments in Hades, he lifted up his eyes and saw Abraham afar off, and Lazarus in his bosom.'* Maybe the image to describe hell in connection with Abraham's Bosom is the former federal prison on Alcatraz Island in San Francisco. Alcatraz sits in the Pacific Ocean surrounded by shark infested water on all sides. You would not be able to escape from it by making a swim for it, nor could you swim to it from any direction. Just as prisoners in Alcatraz could see the city of San Francisco from their prison walls, the rich man in the fiery valley of hell can also see Lazarus in Abraham's Bosom, living in comfort and safety. When Alcatraz was an operating prison, prisoners (comparable to the rich man) gazed at the city from their prison windows and wanted to be there instead of where they were. They were able to see freedom and yet not be able to have it. That would have been torment in and of itself.

"Unfortunately, inhabitants of hell will be separated from the presence of their Creator who made them for fellowship with him, and this means they are there without his blessings and benefits. Without his presence, there is no communion and fellowship with God for eternity. Down here, sin, evil, pain, and suffering are no longer restricted or restrained but can now have free reign and expression. Asking for God's comforting presence will never again be an option. There is no more morning or sunlight, but instead a very grayish black from the smoke and total outer darkness. This outer darkness is the twenty-first torment. Revelation 9:2 says, '*And he opened the bottomless pit, and smoke arose out of the pit like the smoke of a great furnace.* ***So the sun and the air were darkened because of the smoke of the pit.'*** This place is dark because of the smoke of the pit, but more importantly because the light of God's presence is no longer available."

I added another supporting verse of Scripture from Matthew 8:12: '"*But the children of the kingdom will be cast out into outer darkness.*' Being cast into the outer darkness brings the emotional pain of depression because sunlight helps the human body produce melatonin, which keeps the body from getting too depressed. The darkness also invokes more loneliness, fear, trepidation, and anxiety." To offer an example, I asked this question, "Do you remember when you were little, and on a rainy night when there was thunder and lightning outside, you slept alone or with your siblings in your room with the lights out? The only time the room really lit up for a moment was when lightning flashed and showed the shadow from trees outside your window on the walls of your room. It was the darkness that scared you to the point where you wanted to go sleep in Mommy and Daddy's bed just for comfort. Hell is infinitely worse. Only in hell, you won't have God the Father to run to for comfort because his presence is no longer there with you. That would be a type of suffering and pain I would not even want to imagine, let alone experience."

The Twenty-Second Torment

I alerted the tour group to listen up because the rich man was getting ready to respond to Father Abraham in verses twenty-seven and twenty-eight, when it says, '"*Then he said, I beg you therefore, father, that you would send him (Lazarus) to my father's house, 'for I have five brothers, that he may testify to them, lest they also come into this place of torment.'* The rich man is responding to Father Abraham for the first time during this dialogue. This again implies one can talk, breathe, and understand things in hell. This means that down here in hell one still has their sense of hearing, because in order for the rich man to respond to what Father Abraham said, he had to be able to hear and comprehend what was being said. And what he was hearing was continuous weeping and gnashing of teeth—the twenty-second torment. *'But the sons of the kingdom will be cast out into outer darkness.* ***There will be weeping and gnashing of teeth,'*** as we read in Matthew 8:12.

"On our tour of hell we have heard the rich man and others crying, screaming, praying, and pleading for help.

We have heard teeth grinding like finger nails continually scraping against chalkboards. We have heard people calling on Jesus with all sincerity from their hearts. Though we are not experiencing it, all of this commotion is being done at an unbearable pitch. Do you remember hearing a fire engine or an ambulance driving down your street with the siren on very loud? The pitch was so high you had to cover at least one ear so that the sound could be a little more tolerable. Now imagine the sound of millions and millions of people in excruciating pain and suffering responding to being tormented at the same time for all eternity. Even if you did cover your ears, that would not help muffle the sound. The people here in hell are able to understand that they are in a bad situation, and they know while they did not have to be here, this is now their final destination. The worst thing is that it is too late for anyone to help these poor souls."

The Twenty-Third Torment

"The rich man has now accepted the fact that there is no escape from his predicament. There is no going back, so he asks Father Abraham to send Lazarus back to warn his five brothers about this place. This dialogue leads us to the twenty-third torment, which is the desire to warn family and friends about hell, to let them know this is a real place of torture and agony, and to try to get them to stay away. The pain of knowing that those on earth who you love are headed to hell brings untold regrets, including the pain of guilt and shame. If the rich man knew on earth what he now knows in hell, he would have come to Christ and reached out to his five brothers to bring them to faith. But now it is too late, at least for him. This desire to warn family and friends about the reality of hell also brings depression, for hell is a place of psychological and emotional sorrow. These sufferings are on top of and in conjunction with all the other torments. 2 Samuel 22:6 confirms this truth: *'The sorrows of Sheol surround me.'*"

The Twenty-Fourth Torment

I addressed the tour group again and said, "The twenty-fourth torment is found in Isaiah 66:24. *'And they shall go forth and look upon the corpses of the men who have transgressed against Me.* ***For their worm does not die.'*** Mark 9:46-48 says the same thing. 'And if your eye causes you to sin, pluck it out. It is better for you to enter the kingdom of God with one eye, rather than having two eyes, to be cast into hell fire—where their worm does not die and the fire is not quenched.' We have already spoken about the torment of sight, but the twenty-fourth torment in hell is about corpses being eaten by worms that will never die."

Some on our field trip looked like they had questions, so I explained: "People thought Jesus was literally talking about the conscience when the Bible says, *'Their worm does not die.'* But as you can see by looking at the rich man and others, this is not the case. Those in hell will be conscious for eternity. The word *conscience* is used 33 times in the Bible, and in Mark the word refers to a maggot, a worm that preys on dead bodies. The only other time in the Bible that this word is used this way is in Acts 12:23.

God was not willing to share his glory with anyone, and an angel of the Lord killed King Herod because he would not give glory to God. Instead, King Herod claimed to be a god himself, and for this he paid the consequences: *'Then immediately an angel of the Lord struck him, because he did not give glory to God. And he was eaten by worms and died.'* Keep in mind that along with these, there are other insects, bugs, snakes, and awkward looking creepy creatures here as well."

The Twenty-Fifth Torment

I then instructed the crowd to follow me, and after a few minutes we all arrived at the next stop on our tour. "If you look all the way over there you will see locusts, the twenty-fifth torment. Confirmation of what you are seeing is found in Revelation 9:2-3: *'And he opened the bottomless pit, and smoke arose out of the pit like the smoke of a great furnace. So the sun and the air were darkened because of the smoke of the pit.* ***Then out of the smoke locust came upon the earth,*** *and to them was given power, as the scorpions of the earth have power.'*

"Keep in mind that this Scripture is talking about the tribulation period on earth, after the church has been raptured to heaven during the end-times. God opens hell, and out of the smoke come locusts as powerful as scorpions. These ravenous grass hoppers not only reside in hell, but they torment the human souls there, as we can see here on our tour. The phrase '*and to them was given power, as the scorpions of the earth have power'* means that these creatures invoke fear and respect because of how deadly they are. These locusts are unlike the ones we see at our family picnics back on earth, or the ones John the Baptist ate; these are hideous insects, for they have tails like scorpions. Revelation 9:7-10 describes them this way: *'The shape of the locust was like horses prepared for battle. On their heads were crowns of something like gold, and their faces were like the faces of men. They had hair like women's hair, and their teeth were like lions' teeth. And they had breastplates of iron, and the sound of their wings was like the sound of chariots with many horses running into battle. They had tails like scorpions, and there were stings in their tails. Their power was to hurt men for five months.'*"

The Twenty-Sixth Torment

"Now that that part is over, let's continue to move forward and walk down a little further." After walking for a few minutes, we arrived at our next stopping point. "Gather around so I can show you something else. You may not be able to see clearly, but if you look all the way over there it looks like beastly figures tormenting those people. This brings us to the twenty-sixth torment, the demons in hell that torture and torment all those who are here. If you turn around and look back at the fiery chasm, it looks like people in their faint strength are trying to climb out, except that some extremely huge beings are standing around the perimeter pushing them back down in there. Those beings are Satan's demons, the sons of God mentioned in Genesis 6:4. They are comparable to the size of Og, king of Bashan. In Deuteronomy 3:11, we read that their measurements are nine cubits in length and four cubits in width, making them 13 to 15 feet tall, according to the standard cubit. One third of the angels who followed Satan have been delivered into chains of darkness down here to be reserved for judgment. If you look to your right you can see those prison cells with the demons snatching people who come close to the bars. Besides letting us know they are locked up, this means there are prison cells in hell. Since this is the case, this means that the people down here will be tormented and tortured in these prison cells and that there will be demons in the cells with them. The prophet Isaiah supports this truth: *'It shall come to pass in that day that the Lord will punish on high the host of exalted ones, and on the earth the kings of the earth. They will be gathered together, as prisoners are gathered in the pit, and will be shut up in the prison; after many days they will be punished'* (24:21-22).

"Satan has a hierarchical army of demons working for him and running rampant throughout jurisdictions in the world, with God's permission and parameters. If there are demons roaming free on the earth right now, it is certainly the case that those humongous things roaming around free over there are brute demons. Just like the demons attacking and oppressing the people of God on earth, they are attacking and will continue to attack those people over there, who reside here in hell for eternity. The only difference is that down here, God has already given them permission to torture. With no restraints on the suffering they can inflict on those in hell, now there is no limit to what they can do. Demons and every other creature here in hell will torment all who reside here, and they will have an immeasurable level of unmerciful hatred to enable them to continue torturing human souls for eternity. Since God has removed his presence and protection down here, anything goes."

The Twenty-Seventh Torment

"All of the torments in hell will cause terror, trepidation, and fear. But there is one terror that is in a classification all by itself. This brings us to the twenty-seventh torment, the fear of death without being able to die. Those consigned to hell cannot die, because they are already dead. This torment encompasses experiencing what it feels like to be on the edge of death and then death keeps running away for all eternity. 2 Samuel 22:6 says, *'The sorrows of Sheol surrounded me; The snares of death confronted me.'*

The Twenty-Eighth, Twenty-Ninth and Thirtieth Torments

"The last and final known sufferings are the twenty-eighth, twenty-ninth, and thirtieth torments: suicidal thinking, depressed feelings, and abnormal behaviors, respectively. These torments are separate yet very connected. Proverbs 23:7 says, *'For as he thinks in his heart, so is he.'* What this tells us is that thinking has to do with thoughts while the heart has to do with emotions or feelings. Put together, thoughts and feelings produce "so is he," or a behavior. In other words, our thinking affects our feelings, and the combination of the two produces normal or abnormal behavior. Of course down here in hell there are only abnormal behaviors. Some people are tormented by just the thought of committing suicide, and they feel hopeless and depressed. Others not only entertain thoughts of suicide, but they try to carry out the final act of killing themselves. Those existing here in hell experience unimaginable suicidal thoughts, but their attempts at suicide are never successful because they are already dead.

"Once again death keeps running away for all eternity, and no amount of desire to be relieved from the pain will help in any way. On earth, research surveys of suicide survivors reveal that the number one reason people attempt to kill themselves is because they are trying to escape their pain. When asked to be more specific, they expressed that they were trying to escape their psychological, emotional, and physical pain, including in some cases being molested, raped, or abused. What must these torments be like in hell where there is in addition spiritual pain because the presence of God has been removed? The people down here want to die so the suffering will stop. They are hoping and praying desperately to die, but to no avail."

The Tour Winds Down

I tried to spur the tourists' thinking a little further in connection to all that was experienced. "When we think about all the various torments in hell that we have just witnessed, all going on simultaneously, could there be more that we don't know about? How much more unimaginable could the suffering be? Could the same God who created the hideous locust and demons that we just saw actually torment people for eternity? Could he have created more terrifying creatures that have not been exposed yet but will be? Could some of the horrible, sinful acts that take place on earth also take place in hell? Even with all that God has told us in his Word, and all he has shown us here, we do not know all the factors or the extent of the torments of hell. It still remains a vast unsolved mystery. In Deuteronomy 29:29, God has some instruction for us on how we should deal with these mysterious unknown things: *'The secret things belong to the Lord our God, but those things which are revealed belong to us and to our children forever, that we may do all the words of this law.'*

"To add to this, with all that we have seen and heard about hell, I think we all would agree that we have learned enough to know that we don't ever want to come here. Nor would we ever want our loved ones to come here. God would only want us to be concerned about the things that are revealed to us, and he has revealed enough about hell to us today, as well as in his Word, that we might choose to govern ourselves accordingly. If we don't, we have no one to blame but ourselves concerning our final eternal destination." Then I asked our group how they will choose.

"We have covered all thirty torments, and each one of them by itself causes unbearable, unending punishment and suffering. Who could possibly even come close to imagining experiencing all thirty at the same time? While we are on the subject of the number of torments, the fact that God is a God of numerical significance makes the number of notable torments very interesting. If I can explain for a moment, I would start by saying that hell is the most negative place in existence, and I know you all would agree. In connection to hell, the most negative recorded reference to the number thirty in the entire Bible is in Matthew 26:14-16, when Judas, the deceitful disciple, agrees to betray our Lord and Savior Jesus Christ. *'Then one of the twelve, called Judas Iscariot, went to the chief priest and said, 'What are you willing to give if I deliver Him (Jesus) to you?' And they counted out to him thirty pieces of silver. So from that time he sought opportunity to betray Him.'*

"Another verse connected to this passage is found in Zechariah 11:12-14, which says, *'Then I said to them, 'If it is agreeable to you, give me my wages; and if not, refrain.' So they weighed out for my wages thirty pieces of silver. And the Lord said to me, 'Throw it to the potter'—that princely price they sat on me. So I took the thirty pieces of silver and threw them into the house of the Lord for the potter.'* What does this all mean? Well, in verses four through fourteen the prophet Zechariah was instructed to become a good shepherd of the flock and thus enact a prophecy of Jesus Christ. Zechariah was told to feed the flock, even though they were destined for the slaughter, and he was obedient to this. This references Judas' betrayal of Christ and being given thirty pieces of silver, the price of a slave, called by Zechariah a princely price. This was a cheap price and not worth his soul being sent to hell, which was where he ended up because he committed blasphemy. To add to this, the potter referenced in verse thirteen was known among the lowest of society. The ironic and striking similarity between all these details and those relating to the rejection of Jesus Christ makes it plain that Zechariah was making a prophetic reference to Jesus Christ, the Good

Shepherd, and the fate of all those who reject him. When we tie all this together, it means that God has called and commissioned people on earth in the body of Christ to continue to feed and warn those in the world who are destined for the slaughter of hell because they continuously reject the Good Shepherd, Jesus Christ. So all those who rejected the prophet Zechariah were without excuse, paralleling the fact that all those who reject Jesus Christ are without excuse as well. Also, worldly gain like thirty pieces of silver, no matter how expensive, is a cheap, menial slave's price to be given in this life for a soul that ultimately ends up in hell for rejecting Jesus. Judas now realizes that betraying Jesus for thirty pieces of silver was not worth going to hell and experiencing at least thirty notably different revealed torments for eternity.

"On the flip side, the most positive recorded reference to the number thirty in the entire Bible is when Jesus went to the cross. All of this happened in 30 A.D. when he went up a hill called Golgotha (the place of the skull), hung, bled, and died, was buried and rose on the third day with all power in his hands. For all who believe in his finished work, escape the thirty torments of hell and spend eternity in heaven with him. As in the case of Judas, going to hell for rejecting Jesus is just not worth it, not even for the riches of this world and material gain.

"Let me ask the younger people here a question. Have you ever wondered why your parents may be over protective of you? Even though it gets on your nerves, it is because they know what is out there in this hard, cold life and they don't want you to make the same mistakes they made. Their goal is not to get on your nerves or to make life harder for you but to save you a lot of suffering and pain because they have been there, done that, so to speak. It is the same with the rich man here in hell that you have seen. He has been here and will continue to be here unendingly. He just wants to save his brothers the suffering and pain that he is experiencing, but the sad thing is that it is too late. All he can do is hope they get saved while they still have a chance.

"On earth I used to be involved in a prison basketball ministry at my former church. One of the prisons we went to was Fairton Federal Prison, in Fairton, New Jersey. We would play basketball games against real inmates, hoping to build relationships with them through friendly competition. At half time we witnessed and extended invitations for them to come to Christ. Surprisingly, people would raise their hands and admit they were sinners in need of a Savior. They would pray the sinner's prayer and become Christians right there on the bleachers. We showed them a lot of love, and they showed us a lot of love as well." I moved closer to the youth in the tour group and said, "Now listen very closely, young people. When our team got ready to go home, we asked a few of the inmates what advice they would give us to take back to the young people at our church. They said, 'Tell the young people that they do not ever want to come here.' Their painful experience qualified them to speak on this topic, and to try sparing others, just as the rich man was trying to do. As for hell, it is a terrible prison, and you never want to come here, and you never want your friends and family to come here, either. Your choice to receive Jesus Christ as your personal Savior will save you from this fate, and it will spread to your friends and family so they will be spared as well. Okay, let's continue with our tour. We're coming down the final stretch."

Moses and the Prophets

I told everyone we were going to make our way back up the hill near the fiery chasm so we could listen to Father Abraham's response to the rich man. It took about fifteen minutes to walk back up the hill to where we started. When we arrived, I turned to the crowd and said, "Let's listen in on the conversation because Father Abraham is about to address the rich man. Luke 16:29 tell us that 'Abraham said to him, *'They have Moses and the prophets; let them hear them."*

"So once again the rich man's prayer request goes unanswered, just as it was when he cried out, *'Father Abraham, have mercy on me, and send Lazarus that he may dip the tip of his finger in water and cool my tongue; for I am tormented in this flame.'* In saying they have Moses and the prophets, Father Abraham is telling the rich man that his five evil brothers have pastors, preachers, teachers, evangelists, missionaries, and many other Christians, all preaching the gospel of Jesus Christ to them, and all telling them they need to be saved. Nothing else is required.

"But the rich man still tries. In verse thirty, he says, *'No, father Abraham; but if one goes to them from the dead, they will repent.'"* I turned to the tourists once again to offer some comments. "The rich man believes that if Lazarus goes back from the dead he could persuade his five brothers to repent and come to faith in Christ. The rich man exemplifies selfishness, as he did when he was alive on earth. He really wants Lazarus to tell his five evil brothers because he knows they will blame him for leading them to hell, causing him more torment and torture.

"Father Abraham rejects the rich man's request, and he gives this as his reason in verse 31: *'But he said to him, 'If they do not hear Moses and the prophets, neither will they be persuaded, though one rise from the dead.''* In other words, even if he sends Lazarus back from the dead, and even if Lazarus knocks on their door and testifies to them about how real this place is, and even if he tells them of their need for salvation, they still would not believe and come to faith in Jesus. Father Abraham basically is saying that the rich man's five evil brothers and those who have heard the Scriptures have more than enough enlightenment to show them the way to God. No miracle will convince them or any other person who refuses to believe. Anyway, the brothers know Lazarus died and was buried, so they would probably think this was just a joke and that this was not really Lazarus but a look-alike. They probably would think that his burial was a farce. This was certainly the case after our Lord and Savior died, was buried, and rose again. Even with an empty tomb, people still did not believe. Some believed that his body was stolen. This defamatory rumor still circulates to this very day. Jesus even appeared to his disciples and showed them his nailed, scared hands and feet, and some of them still did not believe, at least not at first. Jesus showed himself to hundreds of men, women, and children after he rose from the dead, and most of them still refused to believe."

Back Down the Hill

I told our tour group, "Our field trip is almost over, but we have just one more sight to see before we depart. I must warn you again as I told you earlier that what you are about to see will be unlike anything you have ever seen before. Please follow me, stay together, and I pray God's comfort and peace be upon you for what you're about to experience." We all walked back down the hill to the fiery chasm. When we arrived, I said, "I want everyone to stand near the fiery chasm so you can see, but don't stand too close. Listen carefully and follow my instructions. I want you to grab the hand of the person next to you, and then close your eyes and listen very closely."

All of a sudden, as if someone was slowly turning up the volume on a radio, the tourists began hearing voices. The voices got louder and louder. It sounded like people screaming, yelling, begging, praying, and calling on Jesus and even the tour group. The tourists had their eyes closed, and they began to grip the hand of the person next to them tighter and tighter as they became a little afraid. Listening intently, they thought they could recognize some of those familiar voices. The voices got even louder and they were becoming more clearly recognizable by the members of our party. The sound of sniffling and fast breathing began as they put two and two together. They could hear weeping and the gnashing of teeth. It was at this time that I said to everyone, "Now slowly open your eyes."

An outburst of wailing began among the entire tourist group due to the unendurable sight. Some even fell down on the floor and screamed "Noooooooooooooo," "Oh my God," "Lord, help me, Jesus," "Lord, have mercy on them," "Lord, give them another chance, God," "God, save them, please, I beg you." What they all saw was something they will never forget as long as they live. It was the sight of people they knew in their jobs, in the community, and in their churches. They saw church leaders, church goers, and choir members. They saw celebrities. Sorrowfully, they saw some of their own family members and friends being tormented as they frantically called their names and screamed, "Why didn't you tell me?" There was nothing else to see, and so I announced to everybody, "I'm so sorry. That's it, it's over. We are done and we can go back home now. I know you are devastated by what you just experienced, and I don't know what to say. But we only had an hour for our trip, and our time is up."

Back Up the Hill

I attempted to console the group while the sounds of the voices began to slowly dim until they finally disappeared. Some of the tour members were on the floor crying. The group slowly began gathering composure, and, feeling that they bonded through this experience, they began hugging one another for comfort. I asked everyone to hold on to another's hand and to close their eyes as I closed out the field trip with a short prayer. I simply said,

> *"Dear God, our Father, thank you for allowing us to visit this place called hell without having to stay for eternity. Thank you, Lord, that we*

are on the blessed side of regret today, because if we haven't already, we still have an opportunity to make you our Lord and Savior so that we may spend eternity with you and never have to see this place again. Now continue to comfort us and be with us as we head back to our classroom. In Jesus name and for his sake we pray with thanksgiving. Amen."

We headed back up the hill to the starting point of our field trip. I was in the back of the crowd, and I took one last look at the fiery chasm. What I saw troubled me greatly, for it was a face I thought I knew. Turning and going in the direction of the sight, I saw someone burning in the fire that looked like my grandmother. I could not understand what she was doing down there. It was impossible that she belonged there. I felt sure she was saved. My wife Nikki ran back to me, grabbed my hand, and pulled me away. In an anxious voice she said, "Come on, time is running out and our hour is almost up. We have to go."

CHAPTER TEN

Sudden Turn of Events: More Unexpected Twists

I was standing in front of the class amid pitch black and dead silence. I told everyone to slowly begin to open their eyes. The lights began, dimly at first, to get brighter and brighter. It was like a camera coming back into focus as the class members squinted and blinked and began to regain their vision. Once the lights were completely on, everyone's vision had cleared and they realized they were sitting back at their desks with their Bibles open to Luke 16, where they started their field trip to hell.

All of the sudden as everyone was closing their Bibles and gathering their belongings, they noticed that Ms. Pitts was lying on the floor in the back of the classroom. The workshop participants got up immediately and began to gather around her to help. I was trying to figure out why everybody in the class was rushing to the back of the room. Then I saw Ms. Pitts lying on the floor unconscious and not breathing. I moved quickly to her and could find no pulse. I shouted to Nikki to call 911. I asked everyone to back up so Ms. Pitts could have some air.

Ms. Pitts lay on the floor at the back of the classroom motionless, unconscious, not breathing, without a pulse, and with her eyes closed. I looked at the face of this beautiful lady who lay still on the floor. The rest of the people in the class began to console each other and pray. I fell to the floor and yelled "Noooooooooooooooo, it can't be," and began weeping bitterly over this woman as if at a funeral.

Shortly, the ambulance arrived and they hurriedly began CPR to try to resuscitate Ms. Pitts. They worked while everyone looked on and hoped and waited. After they could do no more to change the situation, the paramedics turned to me, still crying in the corner and praying the entire time. They said they were sorry, but that they had done all they could. Apparently Ms. Pitts had died from a heart attack. They put her on a stretcher, covered her body, pulled a white cover over her face, and then wheeled her out of the classroom and out of the church.

I wanted to console and pray for everyone and make some closing remarks before they left to go home. After a prayer of consolation, I said, "In terms of our field trip, I know what you have just experienced has devastated you. I understand because I am devastated as well. I, too, have family and friends in hell. In fact, the very reason I started doing this workshop and field trip was because of my own family members and friends who reside in hell today. Sadly enough, most of the people I knew down there in hell went there straight from the church. Like the rich man, I want to warn the saved and the unsaved about this very real place of torments. I want to challenge Christians to make sure they are saved, because once it is too late, it is too late. I also want to help us, as Christians, realize the sense of urgency to fulfill the Great Commission, lest many more people will go to that place, not to visit like us, but to stay forever. Ultimately, if Christians step up to fulfill their responsibility for completing the Great Commission, we will all see as many people in the world get saved as possible."

My voice was beginning to crack, and I broke down again as I said to the class: "In all my years of doing this workshop and field trip to hell, this was the worst of them all. Do you remember just before we left hell that I took one last look at the fiery chasm? Do you remember my reaction when I said I saw a woman who looked like my grandmother? That woman was Ms. Pitts, who just had a heart attack and passed away in our classroom." The entire class took a deep breath at the same time. "I regret to inform all of you that as good a woman as she was, Ms. Pitts apparently was not saved. I'm sorry. While we were on our way back, she must have had a heart attack in the classroom while we were finishing up the tour in hell. At the beginning of the class, I asked that if you were not saved to please raise your hands so we could pray with you to receive Jesus Christ as your personal Savior, and no one raised their hands. So before we dismiss, please, for eternity's sake, I want to extend another invitation for anyone to get saved by just slipping up your hands at this time."

The room was very quiet, and without turning their heads, people were moving their eyes to see if anyone would raise their hands this time. I stressed again that everyone must be unequivocally sure they are born again, because once it is too late, it is too late. "You all went on the field trip to hell and saw what it was like firsthand, so therefore all of you are without any excuse now." At that moment, to my surprise, one hand slowly went up, then two, and then three, until out of the sixty-eight people in the room all but seven raised their hands expressing their need for salvation. The room was still and silent when I encouraged everyone who raised their hands by telling them this was the best and most important decision they have ever made in their entire lives.

Deacon Dave Jr. came to the front of the room to go through the Romans Road salvation presentation with all those who raised their hands. Then he had them close their eyes and repeat the sinner's prayer after him. Afterwards, Nikki and I had them fill out some information so the church follow-up team could contact them. Every new Christian needs someone to continue encouraging them through the next steps as they venture in their new walk with the Lord. Lastly, I said, "I want to leave you with a Scripture and a charge before you leave today. Understanding that your growth in Christ is progressive, in Matthew 28:19-20, it says: "Go therefore and make disciples of all nations, baptizing them in the name of the Father and of the Son and of the Holy Spirit, teaching them to observe all things that I have commanded you; and, lo, I am with you always, even unto the end of the age."

I concluded our field trip to hell by saying, "We can't let any more people die and go to hell, especially not straight from the church. We cannot have people continuously coming so close to heaven and not getting in. We need all of you to commit to seeing that this does not happen anymore. Challenge people in love who say that they are Christians to make sure they know for sure that they are saved. Lastly, go tell a dark and dying world that there is a Savior who rescues from the uttermost and can deliver anyone from the fiery pit of hell. He is a Savior who loves them and wants to have a personal relationship with them right now, while changing their lives progressively over time. Once again, I thank you all for coming. God bless you, and remember that Jesus loves you and so do I. You are dismissed."

Everyone got up and began exiting the classroom. As the hallways of the megachurch started filling up with people, one woman was looking at the faces of those coming out of my seminar. She was curious why everyone looked the way they did. She looked at the sign outside the classroom and read that our session was "A Field Trip to Hell." She said to one young man in our group while he was coming out of the class, "From the looks on your faces, I would have thought that you all really went to hell." He stopped, looked the lady in her eyes, and said, "Ma'am, with all due respect, we did go to hell and were blessed enough to be able to come back. I'm telling you that you do not ever want to go there." He walked down the hall with a serious and concerned look on his face while the woman's eyes followed him. She called to him, "If the Word was that good, I think I'll go to this session instead of the original one I signed up for." Not knowing what she was getting ready to embark upon, she walked into the classroom to go on a real field trip to hell.

CHAPTER ELEVEN

Seeing the Big Picture: The Real Focal Point

With all the discussion we have had about God in connection to hell, it is important that we end by seeing the big picture and the real focal point. Sometimes as Christians we can turn people away from the faith in frustration and anger. Why? Not only because of the often evident hypocrisy that we display, just like adherents of all the other religions, but because we claim people are going to hell if they do not believe what we believe. We are heaven-bound, and they are not. It may sound dogmatic and intolerant to portray Christianity as superior to other religions, but saying the teachings of Christ are exclusive is a biblically-supported statement. In Acts 4:12, we read, *"Nor is there salvation in any other, for there is no other name under heaven given among men by which we must be saved."*

We may have only one chance to impact someone for Jesus Christ, and we need to make it count by drawing people towards the gospel and not pushing them away. Which is better, to use the threat of hell to push them away, or the rewards of God's love to draw them in? Some Christians do not even care if they offend people because, "I have to tell them the truth." This attitude has some validity. People do have the right to believe what they choose to believe. But what are the chances of introducing people to Christ when we tell them they are going to hell and do not care if we offend them? The Bible should not be used as a weapon against people, as it sometimes is even against other Christians. As long as someone has met God's requirements for salvation, even with doctrinal differences, we are the body of Christ and God requires that we love one another and be unified. We are to love one another because of the love he demonstrated towards us so undeservingly. In 1 John 4:7-11, John writes, *"Beloved, let us love one another, for love is of God; and everyone who loves is born of God and knows God. He who does not love does not know God for God is love. In this the love of God was manifested towards us, that God has sent His only begotten Son into the world, that we might live through Him. In this love, not that we loved God, but that He loved us and sent His Son to be the propitiation for our sins. Beloved, if God so loved us, we also ought to love one another."* If we want to use the Bible as a weapon to attack someone, then we should use it to attack the real enemy, the Devil, who hates us and our Christian brothers and sisters.

There is an old saying that it is not what you say, but how you say it. This statement is half true and half false, which makes it a total lie. It does matter what you say and how you say it. Of course how we say something is very important because the attitude or spirit behind what we say is crucial. But what we say is very important also. Our choice of words in propounding the gospel may mean the difference between spiritual life and death for others. We want the Good News to be exactly that—good news.

Jesus Died for All

There are many ways to witness or lead someone to Christ other than focusing on hell all the time. If all we can do is threaten people with hell, what happens when, as crazy as this may sound, they are not afraid of hell and it does not scare them? Some people's lives have been so devastated and they have gone through such misfortune in life that they already feel like they have been through hell and back. Some people have lost so much hope in life because of what they have gone through that they cannot wrap their minds around God's love for them. For them, putting all the negative events of their lives in proper biblical perspective is all but impossible. In the final analysis, some people have suffered so much negativity in life that they don't even care about the impending menace of hell. It just does not move them one way or the other.

There are some people who, because of their pessimism and hopelessness, actually think hell is a deserved place for them. They think hell is the destined ending for their life story anyway. Any approach to witnessing to these types of people by emphasizing hell will fall on deaf ears. In fact, if it did anything, it would push people to move in the other direction. The "just-as-long-as-I-told-them-and-now-their-blood-is-on-their-own-hands" kind of approach is of no help to hurting people and no help to the Kingdom of God. These types of hurting people need to be reached and given love and hope because Jesus Christ did not just die for some; he died for all. They need to know they are loved—not threatened. They need to hear a witness in line with a God who is able to heal and restore in spite of the pain. Ultimately, it is the things we do in love that will make the biggest difference in people's lives.

We have to be aware of our approach and use wisdom from God because each person may require a different strategy that does not entail the threat of hell. Now I do believe that in some cases, as led by the Lord, some people need to be approached and told about the consequence of hell in a loving but straightforward way. After all, people come to Christ out of different motives. For some, the incentive of staying away from hell is the thing that brings them into the Kingdom. But that is not true of everyone all the time. Quite the reverse. Furthermore, some Christians purposefully use the threat of hell as a stumbling block to the nonbeliever because it makes them feel better about themselves. It makes them feel more spiritual than others. However, God did not convey the message of the gospel with an emphasis on the possibility of hell but rather based on his love, grace, mercy, and his ability to save.

Live to Influence for Christ Another Day

In order to better minister to someone, it is best if we can try understanding the way they think, feel, and behave. In situations where you can get the heads up, just knowing the signs of the times and the ways of the world will help tremendously. To an unsaved person, or someone of another religious orientation, listening to these types of "you are going to hell" statements made by believers seems closed-minded. Their response, which is a strong argument, is, "With all the religions out there, what makes yours the one I should believe in or else I go to hell?"And if they have seen some not-so-Christ-like evidences in our lives, we will have our work cut out for us. Their response then is, "Who are you to tell me I'm going to hell because I don't believe what you believe?" Another consideration is that "you are going to hell" announcements imply that their family members and friends who have passed away are already in hell (if they did not believe the same thing we believe). This is not something we want to imply when we are witnessing for Christ. When we think of the impact a thought like that would have on any listener, even if it is true, do we really think that it is an effective way to go about building the church? Our chances of winning people to Christ will go from slim to zero. Building the church is all about trying to win someone to the Lord by couching what we say in love.

There is an old saying that goes, "Live to fight another day," which simply implies that we should try keeping our chances at something going rather than ending them. I would like to restate that saying: "Live to influence for Christ another day." It would be better to have the chance to impact someone for Christ in an ongoing way than for them to be turned off and shut down to the gospel because of either our words or our behavior.

To minister in wisdom and knowledge, we Christians should understand how the world thinks, but we should not have worldly thinking. The reason why this is important is so that we might win some. Wisdom tells me that people have the right to believe whatever they choose to believe without someone telling them they are going to hell. But wisdom also tells me that I can lovingly impact and influence those around me with my attitude, behavior, and especially the words I choose to use as I relate to people on a daily basis. In fact, if we focus on this, people will come to us to learn about the hope that is within us because they see something different in our lives. When that happens we should be ready to give an answer. This approach is not only taken when I am directly dealing with someone, but also when I am dealing with them indirectly—when my testimony is being watched and I don't even know it.

The Greatest of These

When trying to win someone to Christ, wisdom tells me to stay far away from the threat of hell and put more emphasis on the love God has for them. He loves them so much that he died on the cross to pay for their sins and desires to have a personal relationship with them right now. We also need to convey to people that our sanctification (the state of growing in God's grace) is progressive, meaning that we change over time, not overnight. The cherry on top of the sundae is that in accepting Jesus as their personal Savior, they now have the benefit of spending eternity in heaven with Christ when this life is over. But with all the talk about the reality of hell, how is a person to be won for Christ and kept from being turned off by the faith, thus being a stumbling block to their salvation? Instead, let us focus on the awesome love that God has for them and the personal relationship he wants them to enter into with him. This is the real focal point. Let people see the love of Christ reflecting in our hearts due to our words, our attitudes, and our behavior. If we do that, witnessing will become a whole lot easier. Paul tells us in 1 Corinthians 13 about the importance of love.

> *"Though I speak with the tongues of men and of angels, but have not love, I have become sounding brass or a clanging cymbal. And though I have the gift of prophecy, and understand all mysteries and all knowledge, and though I have all faith, so that I could remove mountains, but have not love, I am nothing. And though I bestow all my goods to feed the poor, and though I give my body to be burned, but have not love, it profits me nothing."*

Verses one to three talks about how, despite all the gifts of prophecy, tongues, and knowledge that I have, if I do not exercise them in love, it profits me nothing. If when exercising the spiritual gifts they profit me nothing, then they sure do not profit anyone else anything, either.

> *"Love suffers long and is kind; love does not envy; love does not parade itself, is not puffed up; does not behave rudely, does not seek its own, is not provoked, thinks no evil; does not rejoice in iniquity, but rejoices in the truth; bears all things, believes all things, hopes all things, endures all things. Love never fails. But whether there are prophecies, they will fail; whether*

there are tongues, they will cease; whether there is knowledge, it will vanish away."

Verses four through eight talks about the characteristics of love and how all of our gifts of prophecy, tongues, and knowledge are going to fail, cease, and disappear.

"For we know in part and we prophesy in part. But when that which is perfect has come, then that which is in part will be done away. When I was a child, I spoke as a child, I understood as a child, I thought as a child; but when I became a man, I put away childish things."

Verses nine through eleven talks about how in eternity there will be no more need for gifts of prophecy, tongues, or knowledge to build up the body of Christ, and that childish things will be discarded.

"For now we see in a mirror, dimly, but then face to face. Now I know in part, but then I shall know just as I also am known. And now abide faith, hope, love, these three; ***but the greatest of these is love."***

Verses twelve and thirteen are the real focal point of this passage, which is all about God's love.

Spiritual gifts will only have value in this life if they are used to build up faith, hope, and love, because these greater realities have eternal significance. The apostle Paul also lets us know that faith will eventually become sight, hope will eventually become fulfilled, but love, the greatest gift of all, will remained unchanged.

Grace and Mercy Made a Way

Even though heaven and hell are important aspects of this life and the life to come, they are not the most significant aspects. If we were to view God in that way, then we would only see him as a cosmic parent sitting in heaven dictating to us what to do according to his Word—or else. He might send us to our eternal room (hell) where we will remain in punishment for the rest of eternity. Surprisingly, this is the perspective of God that many people have. But God is a God of balance, and this attitude is very far from how he wants us to view him and his Word. The most significant aspect of this life and the life to come is God as a loving parent, willing to give his Son for the sins of the world, and willing to give his Word as it pertains to life

Jesus went through the ultimate suffering when he was crucified on the cross. He can identify with our faults because he was tempted in all the ways we are, and yet he was without sin. Hebrews 4:15 says, *"For we do not have a High Priest who cannot sympathize with our weaknesses, but was in all points tempted as we are, yet without sin."* Some may say, "Jesus was perfect and I'm not," but God knows we are going to fall at times and yet he still loves us. He knows that we are going to sin, but the good news is that his love, grace, and mercy made a way so that our past, present, and even our future sins would be covered by the blood Jesus shed for our sins when he died on the cross. The only requirement for this forgiveness is faith in the finished work of Christ. We will never be sinless. However, God's undeserved love, grace, and mercy is constantly extended toward us and should motivate us to want to sin less than we used to. And even if we do sin, God's love has made a provision for us to repent, be forgiven, and go in the opposite direction of that sin. 1 John 1:9 puts it this way: *"If we confess our sins, He is faithful and just to forgive us our sins and to cleanse us from all unrighteousness."* Why? Because of his awesome love that was demonstrated by Jesus' death on the cross.

Jesus, too, is like the parent who has life experience and wants to leave his Word as instructions for his children because he knows just how much Satan, sin, and the system of the world will hit, hurt, and hinder us. Our parents sometimes said things to us that got on our nerves, but they were trying to tell us for our own good. Why? Because they did not want us to go through the painful experiences they went through. It may not have seemed like it to us at the time, but our parents did it because they loved us. And so it is with God. He does these similar things that we may not always agree with or understand, but he does them because he loves us and wants what is best for us in this life and the life to come.

A Great Romance

The Bible is the greatest "romance" ever written, because it is a story about a God who had no reason to love us but was determined to love us anyway. He demonstrated his love towards us and saved us from our sin and ourselves. He then progressively changed us and used us for his Kingdom and his glory. As God's children we are just as imperfect as our hero characters in the Bible—people like Moses, King David, and the disciple Peter, just to name a few. But he still used them mightily to impact the world and human history, just like he still chooses to use us mightily to impact our times. Why does God do all of this? He does this because he loves us so much. It is really not about God desiring to send any one to hell, because he does not desire this, and anyway, hell is our choice, not his. What it is about is an immeasurable God with an immeasurable love that we did not deserve that should compel us to want to willingly give our hearts, minds, wills, and most importantly our lives to him. This awesome love liberates us to not only want to serve but also to please him and do what makes him happy.

Think of it like this. You got caught red-handed committing a crime. You pleaded guilty because it was obvious you did it, and you were convicted of that crime. Then the judge said that he would let you go free on one condition. He would only let you go free if you received the free gift box in his hand, and if you did, all the charges would be dropped. He said he would do this because he loves you. Being wise and accepting this too-good-to-be-true offer, you approach the judge's bench and he exchanges the free gift box from his hand to your hand, whispers that he loves you, and tells you to return to your seat. Then the judge, who is pleased that you accepted his free gift, smiles at you and announces he has reached his decision. He pronounces you "not guilty," slams down his gavel, and tells everyone in the courtroom to have a nice day. Of course all onlookers in court that day would be puzzled and lost for words. You think the judge is crazy. Why would he do this for you? You wonder what you did to deserve getting off the hook so easily when you were guilty of the crime. If nothing else, you would feel forever indebted to that judge because of what he did for you as a measure of the love he demonstrated to you.

It is the same analogy with God, because we are all guilty, like Adam and Eve's crime of sin, disobedience, and rebellion committed in the Garden of Eden. Deserving of being sentenced to jail in hell for eternity, God extended an opportunity for us to have all charges dropped if we would just receive the free gift of salvation in his hand provided by his Son, Jesus, and his death on the cross. He wants to extend this free gift to us from his hand to our hand—and ultimately our hearts. Upon receiving this free gift of salvation and being declared "not guilty" by God, we should feel forever indebted to live for and serve him because of what he did for us as an immeasurable act of undeserved love. Consequently, it is not just about God's love but also his grace, which is being given loving favor we don't deserve, and mercy, which is not being given the punishment we do deserve. We are engrafted into that love and his loving character. This truly is a great romance.

Greater Love has No One

God does not want to send anybody to hell. He loves us dearly, and we are the apple of his eye. The gospel of John 15:13, says, *"Greater love has no one than this, than to lay down one's life for his friends."* What does this Scripture really mean? Let's look at all three parts of this verse. The first part of the verse is, *"Greater love has no one than this."* That is the adoration or the love part. God is saying that he has a great love for us, and no other love can compare to this type of love he has for us. God has what we all are really looking for in life. The second part of the verse is, *"than to lay down one's life."* That is the action or the life part, where God is saying that he is not only going to tell us about this great love but that he is going to back it up with his actions by demonstrating his love to us by going to the cross. In doing so he was hung high, his arms were stretched wide, and he bled and died when we deserved to be there instead of him. Now that is love. Jesus still has the nail-scared hands, feet, and side to prove it. The third and final part of the verse is, *"for his friends."* That is the affection or the likable part because God views us as his real friends. The thought of the God of the universe calling me his friend is a little moving on the inside, to say the least. When we think about who God is in all of his splendor, majesty, glory, and power, and the fact that he has called us his friends, it should make us feel loved, accepted, and blessed.

The more we understand just how awesome God's vast physical creation is, and the fact that the God of love who created these magnificent things called us his friends, the harder it is to fathom. Not only does it cause our faith to grow, but it also helps us realize just how special we are. The Creator who used earth and all that dwells on it as a display of his artwork thought enough of us personally to call us his friends. How big a loving personal friend do we have? Consider these facts:

- *God put the earth on a twenty-three degree axis, understanding that if it was one degree to the right, on a twenty-four degree axis, all the continents would be frozen today. That God calls us his friends.*

- *God created the earth that is spinning one thousand miles per hour on its axis, and put a principle in place called gravity that helps sustains us so that we do not float away into outer space. That God calls us his friends.*

- *God created the eagle with such keen eye sight that it can spot a field mouse from on top of a mountain perch. The eagle can glide for miles with one flap of its mighty eight foot wing span, and swoop downward at super fast speeds to get that mouse. That God calls us his friends.*

- *God created the school of fish that swim in a synchronized pattern under the water, moving and turning at fast speeds—and they never bump into one another. That God calls us his friends.*

- *God created the cheetah, the fastest land mammal. It can run seventy-five miles per hour and is the only cat with non retractable claws for better traction while trying to catch its prey. God created the same cheetah to have black fur that comes down the insides and under the cheetah's eyes to block the sunlight while chasing its prey. He created the same cheetah by giving it the type of stomach that serves as a thermometer to measure heat and over-exhaustion, and to let the cheetah know that it must move fast to catch its prey. It only has a certain amount of time to catch its prey or it will have to abort the chase due to overheating. That God calls us his friends.*

- *God created a green lizard called a chameleon that can blend in with its environment by jumping on a brown tree for example and turning brown. That God calls us his friends.*

- *God created the Venus flytrap whose mouth is open with nectar sitting on its three hairs in the middle of the mouth, on which flies land to eat. When the fly triggers one hair two times or two hairs at the same time, the trap shuts. That God calls us his friends.*

- *God created geese that instinctively fly in the "V" formation, and who each instinctively rotate being the front leader so that no one bird gets overworked or worn out. That God calls us his friends.*

- *God threw out billions of stars into the universe, told each star where to land, and gave each star a different name. Not one falls without his permission. That God calls us his friends.*

- *God created flowers that produce their own perfume, and the sun that hangs in the sky without a hook. That God calls us his friends.*

- *God created the polar bear, the largest land mammal that can smell food from twenty miles away. That God calls us his friends.*

- *God created the fly fish, that can swim fast enough to propel itself out of the water at twenty miles per hour and, while in the air, flap its fins seventy times per second and glide over five hundred feet before plunging back into the water. That God calls us his friends.*

- *God created the woodpecker that pecks twenty-two thousand times a day and can peck at a rate of twenty-three pecks per second. That God calls us his friends.*

A Place for Us

God's awesomeness goes on and on and on and yet he is still the same God who is able to humble himself to call us his friends. All because he is ready, willing, and waiting to have a personal relationship with us. Sometimes we are waiting on God to do something in our lives, but we need to be alert to the fact that God is waiting on us to come to him by faith. When we think about it like this, even though hell does not totally drop out of the picture, it loses being the focal point as to why we should give our hearts and our lives to an awesome friend like this. Who would not want to willingly live for and serve a great friend like Jesus? And the bonus is that we get to spend eternity in heaven with him in mansions he has already prepared for us. In John 14:2-4, it says: *"In My Father's house are many mansions; if it were not so, I would have told you. I go to prepare a place for you. And if I go and prepare a place for you, I will come again and receive you to Myself; that where I am, there you may be also. And where I go you know, and the way you know."*

Most importantly, we will have communion and fellowship together forever. After having gone through all the pain and suffering that we experienced in life, we can have hope right now, while still here on earth, that one day all of our pain, problems, and persecutions will be no more. God gives us a glimpse of what it will be like when we meet him in heaven in Revelation 21:4-5: *"And God will wipe every tear from their eyes; there shall be no more death, nor sorrow, nor crying. There shall be no more pain, for the former things have passed away. Then He who sat on the throne said, 'Behold, I make all things new.' And He said to me, 'Write, for these words are true and faithful.'"*

What a tragedy it would be to go through all the pain and suffering in this life only to die without Jesus and go through an unimaginable amount of pain and suffering in the life to come. However, it is not the threat of hell that should compel us, but rather a great God who has a great love for us and is waiting every day for us with arms open wide. He will receive us and accept us just as we are. The true focal point is **God's love.** In Revelation 3:20, we read, *"Behold, I stand at the door and knock. If anyone hears my voice and opens the door, I will come in to him and dine with him, and he with Me."* He is knocking right now on the door to your heart. Will you open up the door and let Christ in? Will you give him a chance to extend his love to you today?

CHAPTER TWELVE

The Secure Gift: A New Beginning

I want to leave you with a parting gift in connection with our field trip to hell, but before I do, I want to give you a serious case in point. I will deliver a challenge for a real cause. I will give a confirmation, a closing statement, a concluding caution, and then the concluding gift. All of this will be to spur and compel your thinking, because I care about you, the reader.

The Case

The case is found in Matthew 7:22-23. "Many will say to me in that day, 'Lord, Lord, have we not prophesied in your name, cast out demons in Your name, and done many wonders in Your name?' And then I will declare to them, 'I never knew you; depart from me, you who practice lawlessness!'"

This is arguably the saddest Scripture in the entire Bible. These verses reflect that final moment of truth when the unrighteous are standing before Jesus, who has fire in his eyes as Judge. The phrase *"in that day,"* is referring to Judgment Day for the unrighteous, which can be compared to Revelation 20:11-15. It reads, "Then I saw a great white throne, and Him that sat on it, from whose face the earth and heaven fled away, and there was found no place for them. And I saw the dead, small and great, standing before God, and books were opened. And another book was opened, which is the Book of Life. And the dead were judged according to their works, by the things which were written in the books. The sea gave up the dead who were in it, and Death and Hades delivered up the dead who were in them. And they were judged each one according to his works. Then Death and Hades were cast into the lake of fire. This is the second death. And anyone not found written in the Book of Life was cast into the lake of fire."

At this point, Jesus is fulfilling his role as Judge and has the Word of God opened as the Jury. Also, the Lamb's Book of Life is opened to confirm which names will or will not be found in it. If one's name is listed, they are declared righteous and not guilty, because they have been saved by the blood of the Lamb, Jesus. If one's name is not listed, they are declared unrighteous and guilty. In Psalm 9:17 it says, *"The wicked shall be turned into hell, And all the nations that forget God."*

In the Lord's final verdict, all of the unrighteous whose names are not listed in the Lamb's Book of Life will be sentenced to hell one by one. Some of them will be saying, *"Lord, Lord,"* but they will not be saved, and Jesus will say to them, *"Depart from Me you who practice lawlessness!"* (Matt. 7:23). The key word in this verse is *practice*, because it is referring to a continuous or normal way of life. When one comes to Christ, there is still sin in the life, but the believer cannot practice it because the Holy Spirit will not allow that to happen without interrupting us at some point in our walk. One of the job descriptions of the Holy Spirit is to supervise our progressive sanctification process (the process of growing in divine grace) and even though he may be long suffering toward us, he is definitely committed to our growth and development. So ultimately, in desperation, the unrighteous will try to negotiate their way into heaven by reminding Jesus of their long resume of works and the accomplishments that they did for Jesus. The problem is that they did not belong to Jesus in the first place, which is confirmed when Jesus said, *"I never knew you; depart from Me, you who practice lawlessness!"* The Bible tells us in John 10:3 that Jesus, who is the Good Shepherd, knows his own sheep and calls them by name: "To him the doorkeeper opens, and the sheep hear his voice; and he calls his own sheep by name and leads them out."

In Matthew 7:22-23, the unrighteous, who were not saved, were prophesying in Jesus' name. The word *prophesy* means to proclaim or to preach. We see this example in the iconic passage of Scripture called "The Valley of Dry Bones" in Ezekiel 37:4, which says: "Again He said to me, 'Prophesy to these bones, and say to them, 'O dry bones, hear the Word of the Lord!''' The person who prophesies in most churches would probably be the pastor, or maybe the ministers, deacons, or teachers.

The unrighteous, who were not saved, were casting out devils in Jesus name and, according to these Scriptures, were getting positive results. They did many wonderful works in Jesus name and, once again, according to these Scriptures, were getting good results. Sadly, with all that they supposedly did for Jesus, his response to them was, *"I never knew you so depart from me and be cast into the lake of fire in hell, you workers of iniquity."* When Jesus says, *"I never knew you,"* he means he never knew them in connection to his righteousness. They were never in right standing with him because they were not covered in his blood, and therefore they were not saved. 2 Corinthians 5:21 puts it like this: "For He made Him who knew no sin to be sin for us, that we might become the righteousness of God in Him."

If the unrighteous did not belong to Jesus, then how could they use his name to prophesy, cast out devils, and do many wonderful works? How could they have done all that and gotten positive results? Remember Satan's duplication power. The wheat (the righteous) and the tares (the wicked) exist side-by-side and both will continue growing together so the righteous will not be uprooted when trying to gather up the wicked. This will occur until God calls for his reapers to separate and gather them for the harvest judgment. The unrighteous can do marvelous works also because the power is always in the name of Jesus, not the people who use his name. The name of Jesus never ceases to lose power depending on who is using it, whether they are righteous or not. There is authority in his name, and at the mention of it, something has to change. Something will manifest itself first in the spiritual realm causing a change in the physical realm. The Word confirms that in the name of Jesus sick people get healed. In the name of Jesus the blind are made to see. In the name of Jesus the lame get up and walk. In the name of Jesus the power of sin is broken. And, in the name of Jesus people get saved. That is why the song writer once said, "There is something about that name."

What is it about the name of Jesus? God the Father exalted Jesus and his name because of what he did on the cross. The apostle Paul explains it this way in Philippians 2:8-11: "And being found in appearance as a man, He humbled Himself and became obedient to the point of death, even the death of the cross. Therefore God also has highly exalted Him and given Him the name which is above every name, that at the name of Jesus every knee should bow, of those in heaven, and of those on earth, and of those under the earth, and that every tongue should confess that Jesus Christ is Lord, to the glory of God the Father."

The gospel of Matthew also points out that not only can one do ministry and not be saved, but one can also do ministry with the wrong motives while still getting positive results. Matthew wrote that, "Many will say to Me in that day, 'Lord, Lord, have we not prophesied in Your name, cast out demons in Your name, and done many wonders in Your name?' And then I will declare to them, 'I never knew you; depart from Me, you who practice lawlessness!'" (7:22-23). In the end, those who do ministry in Jesus' name but who still practice lawlessness will not get any credit from God for doing the works that they did. They will go straight to hell from the church.

Another point about Matthew 7:22-23 is that God, who is in control of everything and everybody, can even use the wrong motives of the unrighteous in the scope of his sovereign will and purposes. Even though these people were not among the genuine believers, there were apparently some people who benefited from the works that they did. People were preached to, had demons cast out of them, and many wonderful works were done in the name of Christ. I used to hear my grandmother say, "In heaven, there will be some people that you thought would be there and will not." On the other hand, she would say, "There will be some people who you thought would not be there that will be." It will be the same in the context of hell as well. There are going to be some people who escape hell that will surprise us all. More surprising still, there are going to be a lot of people going straight to hell from the pulpit, the elders and deacons committees, the choir loft and music stations, and the pews.

The Challenge

The challenge is found in Revelation 12:4, 7-8: "His (Satan's) tail drew a third part of the stars (angelic host) of heaven, and threw them to the earth. And the dragon stood before the woman who was ready to give birth, to devour her Child as soon as it was born…And war broke out in heaven: Michael and his angels fought with the dragon (Satan); and the dragon and his angels fought, but they did not prevail, nor was a place found for them in heaven any longer." Satan was intelligent, deceitful, and crafty enough to deceive one-third of the angelic host into leaving their first estate, heaven, to follow him. Keep in mind that before their fallen state, these angels were perfect and had no flaws or sin nature. The entire human race has flaws and sin natures, and Satan uses these things against us by tempting us to disobey and rebel against God. Remember that if Satan convinced the angels, who did not have such weaknesses, he certainly has the ability to deceive us, who are not perfect and have flaws as well as a sin nature. What deceit and craftiness must it take to accomplish that?

Satan took the form of a serpent to deceive Adam and Eve. Eve did not sin because she was deceived, but Adam, on the other hand, sinned willfully because God gave the instructions and responsibility directly to him, not Eve. This is confirmed in 1 Timothy 2:13-14, which says, "For Adam was formed first, then Eve. And Adam was not deceived, but the woman being deceived, fell into transgression." Keep in mind that Adam and Eve were also perfect and had no flaws or sin natures. But now the entire human race has the sin nature, and Satan uses these things against us by tempting us to disobey and rebel against God. If Satan could convince the angels who followed him, and if he could persuade Adam and Eve, none of whom had a sin nature, he has the ability to successfully deceive people into believing that they are righteous and going to heaven—when they are not. Satan's deceptive power is extremely effective.

On Judgment Day there are going to be some people standing before Jesus who ask, "Lord, Lord, did I not answer the altar call? Did I not go up in front of the church in your name? And did I not go into the back room and pray the sinner's prayer in your name?" These poor souls will have been deceived by Satan into thinking they prayed with sincerity in their hearts. This would be a tragedy. God is the ultimate Judge of the motivations of the heart, and he cannot be fooled. Coming close will not work, not when it comes to getting into heaven. He will give them the verdict and they will be cast into the lake of fire. Satan has the ability to deceive people to this degree. Coming so close will not get us into heaven, but it can very easily get us into hell.

The Cause

The cause is found in 1 John 1:6-8. "If we say that we have fellowship with Him, and walk in darkness, we lie, and do not practice the truth. But if we walk in the light as He is in the light, we have fellowship with one another, and the blood of Jesus Christ His Son cleanses us from all sin. If we say that we have no sin, we deceive ourselves, and the truth is not in us."

Once a person has been deceived, for whatever reason, they will live in a state of self-deception unless they are presented with the truth and are willing to receive that truth. In essence, self-deception is adhering to a lie or lies as truth in one's own mind, causing one to feel that the lie is not a lie but instead the truth. The end result is living out lies as truth behaviorally. Proverbs 23:7 gives us some insight on this process when it says, "For as he thinks in his heart, so is he." In this passage of Scripture, "thinks" refers to the mind or one's personal perspective. "Heart" refers to emotions or feelings, and the phrase "so is he" refers to consistently produced behaviors as a result of one's perspectives and feelings respectively. This process holds true for a mind governed by truth as well as for a mind governed by lies and deception.

Distorted perceptions lead to distorted feelings. The combination of distorted perceptions and distorted feelings leads to consistently distorted behaviors. On the other hand, perspectives in line with truth lead to feelings that are in line with truth, and the combination of the two leads to consistent behaviors in line with truth. This is why the truth of God's Word must continuously permeate our minds. We live out behaviorally what we believe.

The word *live* is a derivative of the word *life*. Living life in line with truth causes us to live abundantly. Abundant life is what Jesus came to give us, as John 10:10 shows. "The thief does not come except to steal, and to kill, and to destroy. I have come that they may have life, and that they may have it more abundantly." On the contrary, living life in line with lies causes us to live in a deceived or backwards state because we live going in the opposite direction of God's Word. If you spell the word *live* backwards, it spells *e-v-i-l*. A self-deceived, evil life causes one to live backwards—right becomes wrong and wrong becomes right—not according to the truth of God's Word but according to the truth in one's own mind.

If I were in a classroom full of people and I asked everyone in the class who were Christians to raise their hands, some of the self-deceived people would raise their hands along with the true believers. In their own minds they are saved, but not according to the Word of God. In their own minds they have no need to receive Jesus as their personal Savior because they are self-deceived and believe they are already saved when they are not. Their deceived perspective that they are already saved deceives them into feeling they do not need to turn to Christ.

Being self-deceived can produce behavior that is opposite to the way God desires us to live. Our faulty perspectives eventually influence our faulty behaviors, causing us to walk in the error of our ways. If a person has not prayed the sinner's prayer by faith, however, and meant it with all sincerity from the heart, they have not come to Christ for salvation. Unfortunately, in these cases, if they were to die in their unsaved state, they would stand before Jesus as Judge and be sentence to eternity in hell.

The Confirmation

The confirmation that you are on your way to heaven can be highlighted in the following story. One summer I attended a conference at a megachurch. The youth pastor from the Christian Stronghold Church in Philadelphia was instructing my particular seminar. He said, "I have a true testimony that I would like to share with everyone before we get started. I want everyone to take a deep breath right where you are sitting, and then I want everyone to say the word 'pastor.'" So we all took a deep breath as he had instructed, and then we all said "pastor" in unison. And then he said, "Last week on Sunday there was a pastor who came down off his own pulpit and admitted that he was not even saved. He came to Christ in a genuine way on that day." He then said, "The name of the pastor is not important, but thank God the brother got saved." I could not have agreed with our instructor more, even though I must admit I was in a state of shock.

Think for a moment about the case, the challenge, and the cause that has been presented. Does this story about the pastor not confirm the points? Think about all the midweek Bible studies he may have taught. Think about all the sermons he prepared Sunday after Sunday. Think about how he had prophesied or preached in Jesus' name to the congregation. Think about how he may have challenged people in church to get saved at the end of each of his sermons during the altar call. And yet he was not an authentic believer. Think about how he was getting results as people responded to the Holy Spirit's call to make that long trip down the aisle to get right with God. Think about how God was still using this pastor to do all of this, even though he was not saved at the time. Think about how if he had died "in that day" he would have been one of those who said to Jesus, "Lord, Lord, did I not pastor in your name, and did I not prophesy in your name, and did I not get souls saved in your name?" That pastor would have been hoping that his resume of works would have gotten him into heaven, only to be declared unrighteous by Jesus and hear *"I never knew you: depart from Me, you who practice lawlessness."* He would then be in torment, lifting up his eyes in hell, in the company of the rich man and others who died without true faith in Christ.

Why would this pastor have gone to hell after all the good he did? Because no one goes to hell for what they do (not ignoring that there are consequences for our behaviors), but they go to hell for what they are apart from Jesus Christ as their personal Savior. This should be a wake-up call for the church to make sure our house is really in order, so people will stop going to hell straight from the church.

Could it be possible that you are reading this book right now and are deceived into thinking you belong to Christ and are on your way to heaven? If so, you will be a part of the multitude who will say to Jesus in that day, "Lord, Lord." However, you are on the blessed side of regret today, and the good news is that you still have a choice and a chance to make sure you are delivered from sin and have accepted God's salvation.

The Closing Statement

The closing statement is simply this: If you are born once, referring to your physical birth, you will die twice—physically and then spiritually in hell, which is the second death. If you are born twice, referring to your physical birth, and then born again spiritually through faith placed in the finished work of Jesus Christ on the cross, you will only die once—physically.

As we began with our food for thought, we will end with the same.

If salvation is the requirement to escape hell, and if the Bible is true, then hell is real. If I am a Christian and believe that hell is real, and if you are not a Christian and do not believe that hell is real, in the end I gain and you do not gain if hell does exist. On the other hand, if salvation is *not* the requirement to escape hell and the Bible is *not* true, and I am saved and believe that hell is real and you are not saved and don't believe that hell exists, then we both lose. As I see it, either way you lose twice. The truth, however, is that salvation *is* the requirement to escape hell and the Bible *is* true. Make sure you are saved today because tomorrow just might be too late.

The Concluding Caution

The concluding caution is found in Hebrews 2:1-4: "Therefore we must give the more earnest heed to the things we have heard, lest we drift away. For if the word spoken through angels proved steadfast, and every transgression and disobedience received a just reward, how shall we escape if we neglect so great a salvation, which at the first began to be spoken by the Lord, and was confirmed to us by those who heard Him, God also bearing witness both with signs and wonders, with various miracles, and gifts of the Holy Spirit, according to His own will?" And Joel 2:12-14 says, "'Now, therefore,' says the Lord, 'turn to Me with your heart, with fasting, with weeping, and with mourning. So rend your heart, and not your garments; return to the Lord your God for He is gracious and merciful, slow to anger, and of great kindness; And he relents from doing harm. Who knows if he will turn and relent, and leave a blessing behind Him.'"

The Concluding Gift

The concluding gift is found in Romans 6:23, which reads, "For the wages of sin is death, but the gift of God is eternal life in Christ Jesus our Lord."

First, understand that you are a sinner because of what you are by nature. Second, understand that you need to be saved, especially from yourself. Third, recognize that you cannot save yourself. Fourth, recognize that only Jesus Christ can save you. Last, but not least, accept his free gift of salvation by allowing him to come into your heart. How do you do that? Receiving the gift of salvation is as simple as **A, B, C:**

> **A=Admit.** *Admit you are a sinner by confessing with your mouth that you need God to save you and help you with your life.*

> **B=Believe.** *Believe in your heart that Jesus Christ died on the cross for your sins and that He rose on the third day just for you.*

> **C=Confess.** *Confess Jesus Christ as your personal Lord and Savior.*

"But what does it say? 'The word is near you, in your mouth and in your heart' (that is, the word of faith which we preach): that if you confess with your mouth the Lord Jesus and believe in your heart that God has raised Him from the dead, you will be saved. For with the heart one believes unto righteousness, and with the mouth confession is made unto salvation" (Rom. 10:8-10).

Jesus loves you and invites you to make him your personal Lord and Savior. He wants you to spend eternity in heaven with him. If you want to be sure that you are saved, you are only a heartfelt prayer away. Would you find a quiet place by yourself and repeat this prayer by faith, with sincerity in your heart? It can be done quietly or loudly. Just pray.

Sinner's Salvation Prayer

"Dear Heavenly Father, I am a sinner and I believe that Jesus Christ is the Son of the living God who died on the cross for my sins and rose on the third day. I ask for forgiveness for my sins and I confess you as my Lord and Savior. Come into my heart and change it. Become Lord in my life and Lord of my life. Change me, that I may become more like you. In Jesus name and for his sake I pray with thanksgiving. Amen."

If you sincerely invited Jesus Christ to come into your life and to control your life, you can call yourself a Christian and you can be sure that your salvation is secured for eternity. The Bible says that once you are saved, you are always saved, so you can know you have received a secure gift. The gospel of John confirms the security of the believer's salvation when it says, "And I give them eternal life, and they shall never perish: neither shall anyone snatch them out of My hand. My Father, who has given them to Me, is greater than all; and no one is able to snatch them out of my Father's hand. I and My father are one" (10:28-30).

CONCLUSION

Where Do I Go From Here? I'm Saved: Now What's the Next Step?

First, I want to congratulate you! I believe that if you prayed that prayer with sincerity from your heart that you are now a brother or sister in Christ who will spend eternity in heaven with Jesus and other faithful believers. Then, I want to say welcome to the family of God! You are now his child and you can be unquestionably assured that you are in fact saved. Celebrate your salvation! Since God loves you and created you for fellowship, be sure to join with other Christians for the worship of the Lord.

And remember that God has some good works for you to do here on earth for the advancement of his Kingdom. The counsel of support is found in Ephesians 2:8-10: "For by grace you have been saved through faith, and that not of yourselves; it is the gift of God, not of works, lest anyone should boast. For we are His workmanship, created in Christ Jesus for good works, which God prepared beforehand that we should walk in them."

One of the most frequently asked questions for new Christians is, "Now that I'm saved and belong to the family of God, what do I do next in my walk with God?" I want to give you some useful tips that can help answer this question and help you walk on the path of doing good works that God has created and ordained you to do. When we accomplish those things God has c reated us to do, we can move forward in fulfilling our destiny in Christ. There are some things that new Christians should do immediately, and there are some realities about the Christian life we all need to know.

When someone receives Christ it is a really big deal. It is such a big deal that God's Word tells us that the angels rejoice in heaven over one sinner who repents. In other words, when a person surrenders their heart, obeys the drawing of the Holy Spirit, and receives the free secure gift of salvation by placing their faith in the completed and finished work of Jesus Christ's death on the cross, the angels and all of heaven throw a party because of their excitement. In Luke 15:7, we read this: "I say to you that likewise there will be more joy in heaven over one sinner that repents than over ninety-nine just persons who need no repentance."

We watch Sunday after Sunday as people, sometimes broken, make their way to the altar admitting that they need God. Depending on what church you attend, the church members may clap and cheer "Hallelujah" and say "Amen" as they lift up holy hands to thank God. Why? Because heaven has increased and hell has decreased. A new life in Christ has begun. But now the spiritual war also begins. There is a spiritual boxing ring bell that sounds "Ding, Ding," and spiritual babes in Christ are unknowingly in the spiritual fight for their lives. There are some major problems that tend to present themselves at this juncture and begin to exist for the new child of God.

Some trials can lead the new Christian to quit the Christian walk and go back into the world due to the difficulty of this spiritual warfare. Some tribulations can make the new babe in Christ even doubt his or her salvation because of personal failures in the faith, despite knowing that God's Word says that salvation is secure. To add to this, Satan, our arch enemy, knows very well that a new convert is only a spiritual babe in Christ and is not fortified in the faith just yet. We do not have to fear these things, because God has our back and everything around us. But Satan will throw everything but the kitchen sink at the new child of God to try to discourage him or her early on in the Christian life. His goal is to try making them quit by feeling that they made a big mistake in getting saved. Many new and, for that matter, seasoned Christians have admitted that they had more problems after coming to God than before, when they were in the world. This is not completely true, for we know they did have many problems before coming to God, with the biggest one being that they were destined for hell. The difference is that when they were not saved (or in the world), they were blinded to their own messed up state and were not enlightened spiritually about their condition without God, like they are now. More than this, Satan will use the sin nature and personal issues against them, not to mention the worldly system. He will even use himself against every child of God, but he especially likes to go after the new converts.

We need not be afraid of spiritual warfare because we already have the victory in Jesus Christ. It is worth remembering that we as Christians do not fight for the victory; we fight from a position of victory because of what Jesus Chris's death on the cross not only accomplished but finished. If anyone ever gets tempted to doubt our sure victory, they can fast-forward to the end of our story in the Bible—in the book of Revelation—and find out that we win in the end. However, this is spiritual warfare, and in our Christian walk we win some battles and we lose some. But no matter if we win, lose, or draw, God uses it all to strengthen and develop our faith and our character. He uses the good, the bad, and the ugly to make us more Christ-like. He uses the ups and the downs and everything in between, as well as our failures and our successes, to develop in us a faith of gold as he progressively moves us forward throughout our growth and development process. We must remember that spiritual growth and development take time, even years, and we change over time and not overnight. So hang in there and don't quit because you can do it, and more to the point, God can do it. "He is able to do exceedingly abundantly above all that we ask or think, according to the power that works in us" (Eph. 4:20).

Back to one of the most frequently asked questions for new Christian converts: Now that I'm saved and belong to the family of God, what do I do next? Asked another way, where do I go from here, and can someone show me how to get there? I want to end this book with the beginning steps to this process, and give some practical encouragement to make your spiritual transition better and a little easier.

Important Notes

Look below at the practical steps you can take to make your new walk with Christ a smooth transition. Start the process at the step that applies to you and your specific situation, and appropriate the steps you need that you may have missed. As you go through the process, understand that your spiritual growth and sanctification is a progressive process. In other words, we do not change all at once, but rather gradually.

Don't get discouraged when you sometimes struggle in your new faith in Jesus Christ. Keep at it. You are becoming what he wants you to become. Remember that we are all works in progress. If that weren't the case there would be no need for God's help.

Last but not least, remember that God loves you, and don't ever question or doubt that love or your salvation.

Some Practical Steps You Can Take

1. *Get yourself a good study Bible that you can understand, and read it on a daily basis.*
2. *If you are just starting out reading the Bible, it is recommended that you begin by reading Matthew, Mark, Luke, and John first, but preferably the book of John, so that you can learn more about who Jesus is.*
3. *Make an attempt to study the Word of God as you would if you were in a Bible study course.*
4. *Meditate on Scripture the same way you would as if you were worrying about a problem.*
5. *Memorize Scripture the same way you would as if you were preparing to take a test.*

6. *Lean and depend daily on the power of the Holy Spirit to help you obey the Word, and do not get discouraged about inevitable failures.*
7. *Put God first in your life by setting aside some daily quiet time to read the Word and pray, even if you feel that you don't understand much of the Bible or don't know how to pray eloquently. Just speak from your heart like you would to a best friend, because Jesus is just that.*
8. *Let the Lord lead you to visit and join a loving local church body to build on your Christian experience. Make it a church where the Word of God is preached and that you can attend regularly.*
9. *Make an appointment to talk with your pastor, or youth director, or some other spiritual church leader. Let them know about your salvation experience and your desire to get baptized while humbly submitting to their authority.*
10. *If you are a new convert, attend a new member's orientation in your church, if one is available. Learn more about what the church has to offer.*
11. *Start and finish your discipleship classes so you can learn about your church's doctrinal*

positions and receive the right hand of fellowship when you complete them. In most denominations, this will make you a full-fledged member of your church.

12. *Attend the mid-week Bible Study regularly at your church so you can continue growing and developing spiritually in your Christian walk and in the Word of God.*
13. *Participate in church fellowships regularly so you can surround yourself with good Christian company and partake of the benefits of Christian fellowship.*
14. *Get involved in at least one age-appropriate and/or gender-appropriate ministry in order to grow with other believers on your level, as well as to develop accountability. Some examples would be a men's ministry, women's ministry, youth ministry, young adult ministry, singles ministry, senior's ministry, ministry to street people, sports ministry, and so on.*
15. *Talk to a church leader about finding out your spiritual gifts. We all have them, and we need to use them for service in ministry.*
16. *Get involved with volunteering and faithfully serve in at least one ministry.*
17. *Make a heartfelt commitment to support your church financially.*

18. *Bless the church with whatever talents you may have that can be used for God's Kingdom and to bless others.*
19. *Be loyal in prayer, and bless your pastors and serve them and your church faithfully and consistently.*
20. *Make a commitment to pray for your family and your church family, including the church leadership.*
21. *Don't be afraid to share your faith, even if all you know is John 3:16— "For God so loved the world that He gave His only begotten Son, that whoever believes in Him should not perish but have everlasting life." Just hand out tracts if you want to make a start. All witnessing matters.*

If you will do these things faithfully, I believe that in due time it will be amazing what God uses you to do for his Kingdom—and how he uses you to impact those in your immediate circle of influence. 1 Corinthians 2:9 says it this way: "But as it is written: Eye has not seen, nor ear heard, Nor have entered into the heart of man The things which God has prepared for those who love Him."

Just think for a moment about the fact that you are destined for greatness in Christ, and it all started with a little field trip to hell. God Bless you and your family, and even if I don't know you, I love you with the love of the Lord Jesus Christ. Be encouraged, be blessed, and be a blessing.

ABOUT THE AUTHOR

Being an ex-professional basketball player, and having served as an associate minister, a youth and young adult pastor, and a recreational director, all of Kevin Benton's experiences have led him to having a broken heart for those who do not know Jesus Christ as their personal Savior. He knew God was calling him to do something special to impact the world because of the zeal the Lord gave him at an early age. God had some special assignments for him and he has learned along the way that God sovereignly allows pain in our lives to push us towards our destiny. Kevin and his wife, Nikki, currently minister in their local church and community by lovingly developing, discipling, encouraging, and nurturing people in God's Word. They have found nothing greater in life than being in God's direct will and being used mightily by him to touch the lives of people for Jesus Christ.

KBM

Kevin Benton Ministries
visit our web site at:
www.KevinBentonMinistries.com
or
e-mail us at:
Kevin@KevinBentonMinistries.com

CPSIA information can be obtained at www.ICGtesting.com
Printed in the USA
LVOW08s2231160816

500680LV00001B/179/P

9 781935 986058